What Others Are Saying About This Book

"What a fantastic tool! Every call center management professional should have a copy on their desk. Once again, ICMI has taken what can be an incredibly confusing mess and simplified it."
Eric Burton, *Vice President, Customer Care, Time Warner Cable*

"Breathes life into the mountain of call center jargon. A must-have desktop reference for any call center manager or professional."
Book Booker, *Senior Vice President, Customer Service Division, SunTrust Bank*

"At last, a practical and long-needed book for understanding call center lingo. In a profession awash with acronyms and technical jargon, the *ICMI Call Center Dictionary* is an indispensable tool for staff, managers – anyone who wants the inside scoop on call center terminology."
Keith Bailey, *Co-Founder, Sterling Consulting Group; Co-Author,* Customer Service for Dummies *and* Online Customer Service for Dummies

"This book provides a common language for communication within the call center industry. The definitions are precise, and the book is a valuable resource for anyone who wants a clearer understanding of call center terminology. An excellent job!"
Steve McCabe, *Call Center Manager, KeySpan Energy*

"In a profession that is becoming increasingly international it's great to have a comprehensive listing of those everyday (and not so everyday) terms we all encounter."
Ann-Marie Stagg, *Contact Centre Director, CitiFinancial Europe; Chair of the Call Centre Management Association (UK)*

"This comprehensive book covers A through Z and everything in between... The most interesting and informative compilation of technical and management terminology targeted to those of us in the industry."
Nancy Allen, *Vice President, Wescom Credit Union*

"Who knew that a dictionary could provide so much information? This is the ideal keep-at-your-elbow resource every call center professional needs."
Shelley Elkins, *Director, Global Consumer Communications, Estée Lauder Companies*

"Reduce the 'train and explain' exhaustion with others in the company. Look up the term and let the 'Dictionary' do the work."
Lani Delaney, *Vice President, North American Sales & Customer Service Centers, Club Med*

What Others Are Saying About This Book

"This latest reference work fills another gap in our ever-expanding and dynamic industry by giving our unique environment its very own dictionary. This comprehensive dictionary is a MUST HAVE for every call centre professional."
Hillel Benedykt, *Chief Executive Officer, Callscan Australia*

"This is the official dictionary of the contact center industry – an excellent resource for those new and old to the wonderful world of contact centers."
Fredia Barry, *President, CIAC*

"This A-to-Z guide applies to both private-sector and government call centers as it addresses a full scope of topics... More than just a dictionary, it provides detailed information on the concepts and terminology most critical to world-class call centers."
John Sulenta, *Call Center Manager, California Franchise Tax Board*

"The dictionary is a great and very complete tool to understand the contact center business. Defines all data, technical aspects of a center as well as all areas that touch the internal and external customer... It's really a right hand of any contact center administrator."
Wanda Lopez, *Contact Center Director, Centennial de Puerto Rico*

"In twenty years of running call centers, ICMI methodologies in training were the best I have experienced; *ICMI's Call Center Management Dictionary* is another great resource."
Craige Howlett, *Manager, Stanford Call Center Operations, Communications and Networking Services, Stanford University*

"I've heard it said that a problem well-defined is 50% solved. What a tremendous help this dictionary is to help you move forward when looking at solutions to a problem area."
Donna Parker, *Parker Consulting Services; Current President, Society of Telecommunications Consultants.*

"The conversations of call center professionals are littered with acronyms and jargon that the neophyte must wade through. This dictionary makes that process faster and easier with simple, plain language definitions that are comprehensive in their explanation."
Ralph Rathburn, *Operations Division Manager, Oak Lawn Marketing Inc., Japan*

"*ICMI's Call Center Management Dictionary* is a first class work and a much-needed tool for codifying and standardizing the technical language

What Others Are Saying About This Book

of this important working environment."
Ron Zemke, *President, Performance Resear*
of the Knock Your Socks Off Service *book ser*

"Whatever your position within the call centre, this dictionary will be of practical benefit to you in your everyday role. I believe this dictionary will become the 'de facto' reference book for terms and abbreviations in the call centre industry."
Alan Vaughan, *Managing Director, Call Centre Consultants (U.K.)*

"Finally, a comprehensive source for people to utilize in understanding terms and phrases that surround the call center industry. Until now we had no single source to help them understand the complexities of this industry."
Paul Hebner, *President, Contact Enterprises.*

"All professions, especially those in publishing and training, rely on a number of vital knowledge tools to communicate eloquently and effectively. *ICMI's Call Center Management Dictionary* has taken its rightful place alongside a Thesaurus and Punctuation Guide as a crucial aid in helping keep our ideas and content fresh and relevant."
Dominick Keenaghan, *President, INSIGHTS; Publisher,* Telephony Middle East Magazine

"Communications is the central aspect of this industry and all too often our worst asset. *ICMI's Call Center Management Dictionary* will go a long way toward insuring that we are speaking the same language."
Cynthia Ward Jeffries, *former Director, National Call Center, Federal Communications Commission*

"A comprehensive Dictionary that can be used in the traditional way, but at the same time, an interesting book that attracts your attention. If you read it this way, you start in A and can't stop until Z. The reason is simple: Brad's instructive style and authority is throughout the book."
Eduardo A. Laveglia, *Executive Director, Proaxion- Argentina*

"Where was this book when I was first managing call centers? Every acronym, technical definition and call center management theory is clearly and practically defined in the book. I can't wait until all of my managers have a copy on their desks. Excellent!"
Barry Spiegelman, *Chief Customer Officer, The Beryl Companies*

"If you are interested in providing a valuable tool for your call center associates and managers, this is the book to get. It provides a remarkably

thorough resource of call center acronyms, abbreviations and terms that are utilized in our field on a daily basis."
Kim Daftari, *Director, Network Services, Blue Cross of California/Wellpoint*

"This is our industry's very own 'Call Centers for Dummies' which, by the way, includes everyone, senior and junior, with years of experience, or new to the call center. It provides clarity and the basis on which to discuss what is right for your business."
Sarah Kennedy, *Partner, Service Quality Measurement Group, Inc.*

"The contact center industry is evolving rapidly before us. As new technologies and information emerge, it's often difficult to keep up with terminology and apply it to your environment. This is a comprehensive resource for all contact centers -- an excellent tool that can be put to use everyday in the contact center!"
MaryAnn Monroe, *Project Officer for Quality, National Cancer Institute, Cancer Information Service*

"A long-needed and valuable reference that should be on the desk of anyone who operates or supports call centers."
Ian Angus, *President, Angus TeleManagement Group*

"Some call center industry terms sound like a foreign language... and *ICMI's Call Center Management Dictionary* is an awesome translator! If you're looking for comprehensive resources to help you understand the call center business, this dictionary and *Call Center Management on Fast Forward* are highly recommended. Especially when you begin your journey implementing or transitioning to a call center."
Deborah McGlennon, *Department of the Navy, Call Center Program Specialist*

"*ICMI's Call Center Management Dictionary* is an excellent resource for anyone who works in a call center environment. It offers concise definitions as well as easy cross-reference to the ever-expanding call center language. I wish I had something like this when I started in operations!"
Macauley Nash, *Care Operations Manager, AT&T Wireless*

"Brad Cleveland did it again: this book is another indispensable tool for call center professionals."
Henk Verbooy, *Chief Editor, CallCenterMagazine, Netherlands*

ICMI's

Call Center Management

DICTIONARY

The Essential Reference for Contact Center,
Help Desk and Customer Care Professionals

Brad Cleveland

Published by:
ICMI, a registered trademark of Think Services,
a division of United Business Media, LLC
102 South Tejon, Suite 1200
Colorado Springs CO 80903 USA
www.icmi.com

NOTICE OF LIABILITY

TRADEMARK NOTICE

Copyright 2003 by ICMI
Second printing 2003
Forth printing 2007
Fifth printing 2008

Printed in the United States of America

ISBN 0-9659093-5-2

ICMI's
Call Center Management
DICTIONARY

The Essential Reference for Contact Center,
Help Desk and Customer Care Professionals

Brad Cleveland

United Business Media

Father. fa·ther (fä'*th*ər) *noun.* A man who begets, nurtures or raises a child.

This book is dedicated to my father, Doug Cleveland, who encouraged me to go into this profession. And he was (and still is) always there for me.

Acknowledgements

This project would not have been possible without the contributions of many people. Many thanks:

To my colleagues at ICMI who contributed research and definitions (either directly or to related ICMI publications from which some definitions are drawn): Rebecca Gibson, Debbie Harne, Ted Hopton, Jay Minnucci and Tim Montgomery. Debbie Harne also played a key role in the review and edit process. Also, to Susan Hash for reviewing and editing the manuscript, and to Ellen Herndon for spearheading the design and production of the book – a big thanks to both of you!

To Lori Bocklund, Don Van Doren and the team at Vanguard Communications Corp., and to John Goodman, Cynthia Grimm and the folks at TARP – a variety of terms come from, or are based on, seminars, publications and other joint initiatives with them. They are true professionals. Also, Dr. Don McCain contributed to the ICMI handbook/study guide series (referenced in "Sources"), from which some terms come.

To those who reviewed the dictionary in advance and provided comments and suggestions: Nancy Allen, Ian Angus, Keith Bailey, Fredia Barry, Hillel Benedykt, Book Booker, Eric Burton, Chris Cunningham, Kim Daftari, Lani Delaney, Shelley Elkins, Laura Grimes, Paul Hebner, Craige Howlett, Dominick Keenaghan, Sarah Kennedy, Eduardo A. Laveglia, Wanda Lopez, Steve McCabe, Deborah McGlennon, MaryAnn Monroe, Mary Murcott, Macauley Nash, Cheryl Odee Helm, Donna Parker, Martin Prunty, Ralph Rathburn, Barry Spiegelman, Ann-Marie Stagg, John Sulenta, Alan Vaughan, Henk Verbooy, Cynthia Ward Jeffries and Ron Zemke.

To our clients and seminar attendees over the years. We are grateful for the opportunities we've had to serve you. You have shared so much, and stretched our thinking and understanding.

To Linda Harden, and our entire customer service team at ICMI, for all you do – day in and day out – to make this and other projects possible. Each of you has helped to make ICMI the exceptional company it is! Thank you so much.

Most of all, to my wife Kirsten and our new bundle of joy, Grace (born August 2002). Your love and support make each day a wonderful journey!

Table of Contents

ICMI's

Call Center Management
DICTIONARY

The Essential Reference for Contact Center,
Help Desk and Customer Care Professionals

Brad Cleveland

Introduction

Like most professions, the call center industry has an overabundance of unique terms and acronyms. But those of us in the call center world seem to have done an especially notable job of confusing things. We can't even agree on whether it's called... well, a "call center" – see page 28. (Here, we use the term call center as the generic reference to any customer contact or customer interaction environment.)

Terms vary by country. They vary by supplier. And they vary by organization. More seriously, some terms are used interchangeably when, in fact, they refer to very different things; for example, "occupancy" (p. 127) and "adherence to schedule" (p. 10).

There are some great rewards when you equip yourself and your management team to cut through the clutter and confusion. You will be able to communicate more effectively, make better decisions, get more from educational resources, produce better results and enjoy an advantage in building your careers. In each of these ways, I hope this book is useful.

I believe call centers will play a more important role than ever in coming years. New channels of communication, fast-evolving customer expectations, competitive pressures and economic uncertainties – all of these forces are creating an environment in which call centers are essential to an organization's success. They have become multimedia hubs of communication in a communications-driven economy.

With that, I'll admit to an even higher ambition – that this book helps you enjoy this diverse and fast-evolving profession. Customer behavior, human resource management, information technology, reporting, analysis, research and development, coaching, queuing theory, marketing, forecasting, training, statistics, process improvements, organizational design, teams, communication skills, finance, strategy – hey, whatever your area of interest, you'll find a need for it in the call center. There is truly no other environment like it!

Spelling, grammar and terms are largely based on the U.S. market. If you are located elsewhere, please forgive the American idiosyncrasies. But with that said, this is truly a global profession, and the *Dictionary* is designed to be useful wherever you are located. Even though languages, cultures and missions vary widely across the global call center landscape, I've been amazed over the years at just how similar call centers are on a fundamental level.

This book is designed to be a practical reference. Whatever your role – be it in the call center, in a support role or as a supplier to call centers – it is focused on the things you encounter when developing and operating call centers – the issues related to people, processes, technologies and strategies. If we've overlooked any terms or if there are terms that you

Introduction

believe are inaccurate or unclear, please let us know. (If we include them in the next edition, it's worth a complimentary book!) Good luck, and best wishes.

Brad Cleveland
Annapolis, Maryland
bradc@icmi.com

ACD	Automatic Call Distributor
ACS	Automatic Call Sequencer
ACW	After-Call Work
ADA	Americans with Disabilities Act
AHT	Average Handling Time
AHT	Average Holding Time on Trunks
ANI	Automatic Number Identification
API	Applications Programming Interface
ARS	Automatic Route Selection
ARU	Audio Response Unit
ASA	Average Speed of Answer
ASCAP	American Society of Composers, Authors and Publishers
ASCII	American Standard Code for Information Exchange
ASP	Active Server Page
ASP	Application Service Provider
ASR	Automatic Speech Recognition
ATA	Average Time to Abandonment
ATB	All Trunks Busy
ATM	Asynchronous Transfer Mode
AWT	Average Work Time
BIC	Best In Class
BOC	Bell Operating Company
BRI	Basic Rate Interface
BRM	Business Relationship Management
CBT	Computer-Based Training
CCR	Customer-Controlled Routing
CCS	Centum Call Seconds
CDR	Call Detail Recording
CD-ROM	Compact Disc Read-Only Memory
CED	Caller-Entered Digits
CGI	Common Gateway Interface
CIM	Customer Interaction Management
CIO	Chief Information Officer
CIR	Customer Interaction Recording System

Acronyms and Abbreviations

CIS	Customer Information System
CIS	Customer Interaction Software
CLEC	Competitive Local Exchange Carrier
CLI	Calling Line Identity
CMS	Call Management System
CO	Central Office
COM	Component Object Model
CORBA	Common Object Request Broker Architecture
CPE	Customer Premises Equipment
CRM	Customer Relationship Management
CSR	Customer Service Representative
CTD	Cumulative Trauma Disorder
CTI	Computer Telephony Integration
DAT	Digital Audio Tape
DCOM	Distributed Component Object Model
DDD	Direct Distance Dialing
DDE	Dynamic Data Exchange
DID	Direct Inward Dialing
DN	Dialed Number
DNIS	Dialed Number Identification Service
DSL	Digital Subscriber Line
DTMF	Dual-Tone Multifrequency
ECRM	Electronic Customer Relationship Management
EDA	Economic Development Agency
EIM	Enterprise Interaction Management
ERM	Enterprise Relationship Management
ERMS	Email Response Management System
ERP	Enterprise Resource Planning
EWT	Expected Wait Time
FCC	Federal Communications Commission
FLSA	Fair Labor Standards Act
FMLA	Family and Medical Leave Act
FTE	Full-Time Equivalent
FX	Foreign Exchange Line

GOS	Grade of Service
GUI	Graphical User Interface
HR	Human Resources
HTML	Hyper-Text Markup Language
HTTP	Hyper-Text Transport Protocol
HVAC	Heating, Ventilation and Air Conditioning
ICR	Intelligent Character Recognition
IEEE	Institute of Electrical and Electronics Engineers
IETF	Internet Engineering Task Force
II	Information Indicator
ILEC	Incumbent Local Exchange Carrier
IM	Instant Messaging
IP	Internet Protocol
IRR	Internal Rate of Return
IS	Information Systems
ISDN	Integrated Services Digital Network
ISO	International Organization for Standardization
ISP	Internet Service Provider
IT	Information Technology
ITU	International Telecommunications Union
IVR	Interactive Voice Response
IWR	Interactive Web Response
IXC	Inter-Exchange Carrier
JTAPI	Java Telephony Applications Programming Interface
KB	Knowledge Base
KPI	Key Performance Indicator
LAN	Local Area Network
LCD	Liquid Crystal Display
LEC	Local Exchange Carrier
LED	Light-Emitting Diode
LWOP	Leave Without Pay
MAC	Moves, Adds and Changes
MACRS	Modified Accelerated Cost Recovery System
MBWA	Management By Walking Around

Acronyms and Abbreviations

MGCP	Media Gateway Control Protocol
MIS	Management Information System
MTBF	Mean Time Between Failure
NANP	North American Numbering Plan
NCC	Network Control Center
NFAS	Non-Facility Associated Signaling
NIC	Network Interface Card
NPA	Numbering Plan Area
NPV	Net Present Value
NSP	Network Service Provider
OCR	Optical Character Recognition
ODBC	Open Database Connectivity
OJT	On-the-Job Training
OLAP	Online Analytical Processing
OLE	Object Linking and Embedding
OLTP	Online Transaction Processing
OMG	Object Management Group
ORB	Object Request Broker
PABX	Private Automatic Branch Exchange
PBX	Private Branch Exchange
PC	Personal Computer
PCP	Post-Call Processing
PDA	Personal Digital Assistant
PI	Profitability Index
POP3	Post Office Protocol 3
PRI	Primary Rate Interface
PSC	Public Service Commission
PSN	Public Switched Network
PSTN	Public Switched Telephone Network
PUC	Public Utility Commission
PVIF	Present Value Interest Factor
QOS	Quality of Service
RAD	Recorded Announcement Device
RAN	Recorded Announcement

RBOC	Regional Bell Operating Company
RFI	Request for Information
RFP	Request for Proposal
RFQ	Request for Quote
RISC	Reduced Instruction Set Computing
ROA	Return on Assets
ROI	Return on Investment
ROS	Return on Sales
RSF	Rostered Staff Factor
RSVP	Resource Reservation Protocol
SBR	Skills-Based Routing
SFA	Sales Force Automation
SGML	Standard Generalized Markup Language
SIP	Session Initiation Protocol
SLA	Service Level Agreement
SMDI	Simplified Message Desk Interface
SMDR	Station Message Detail Recording
SMTP	Simple Mail Transfer Protocol
SNMP	Simplified Network Management Protocol
SOHO	Small Office Home Office
SQL	Structured Query Language
SS7	Signaling System 7
TAPI	Telephony Applications Programming Interface
TBT	Technology-Based Training
TCP/IP	Transmission Control Protocol/Internet Protocol
TSAPI	Telephony Services Application Programming Interface
TSF	Telephone Service Factor
TSR	Telephone Sales or Service Representative
TTS	Text-to-Speech
UCD	Uniform Call Distributor
URL	Uniform Resource Locator
UUI	User-to-User Information
VDT	Video Display Terminal
VOIP/VoIP	Voice over Internet Protocol

Acronyms and Abbreviations

VPN	Virtual Private Network
VRU	Voice Response Unit
VXML	Voice Extensible Markup Language
WAN	Wide Area Network
WAP	Wireless Application Protocol
WATS	Wide Area Telecommunications Service
WFMS	Workforce Management System
WWW	World Wide Web
XML	Extensible Markup Language

0345 Number. A telecommunications service in the United Kingdom; the caller is charged local rates and the organization pays additional required charges (installation, rental and usage/distance charges).

0800 Number. The equivalent of a North American 800 number, used in many countries outside North America for toll-free access.

1A2. A basic key telephone system. See Key Telephone System.

24x7. Refers to operations that are always open for business (24 hours a day, seven days a week). Often pronounced "twenty-four seven."

2500 Set. A basic touchtone telephone set. See Dual-Tone Multifrequency.

360 Evaluation. Also called a 360-Review. A performance review that incorporates assessments from managers, peers, direct reports and oneself. These perspectives are compiled to identify strengths and weaknesses.

360 Review. See 360 Evaluation.

500 Set. A basic rotary-dial telephone set. See 2500 set.

5ESS. A central office switching system. See Central Office.

800 Portability. See Number Portability.

802.11b. A set of standards for wireless services.

900 Service. A pay-per-call service where the caller pays a premium charge for the service (e.g., to reach technical support, entertainment services, weather or information lines). Although some viable services exist (e.g., per-incident technical support lines), 900 service developed a stigma from unscrupulous businesses that provided minimal services for exorbitant charges, and is now strictly regulated in most countries.

Abandoned Call (Inbound). Also called a lost call. The caller hangs up before reaching an agent. Abandoned calls are calculated as percent abandonment rates using one of the following two formulas:

1. All calls abandoned ÷ (all calls abandoned + all calls answered)
2. Calls abandoned after objective ÷ (calls abandoned after objective + all calls answered)

Abandoned calls are available directly from ACD reports. Abandonment rate, though often a primary objective, is not a concrete measure of call center performance because it is driven by caller behavior, which the center cannot directly control; it should be of secondary importance to service level. Related terms: Abandoned Rate (Outbound), Caller Tolerance, Service Level.

Abandoned Rate (Inbound). See Abandoned Call.

Abandoned Rate (Outbound). In a predictive dialing mode, this is the percentage of calls connected to a live person that are never delivered to an agent. If no agent is available when the phone is answered, the person called hears silence (or the outbound version of a "please hold" message) and often hangs up. Related terms: Abandoned Call (Inbound), Caller Tolerance, Dialer.

Access Charge. Fees paid for the use of a line provided by a telephone company.

Account Code. A code assigned to a specific project, division or client. When making an outbound call, account codes can tie costs back to specific projects.

Action Plan. A list of actions or activities (tactics), which are intended to lead to desired results.

Active Server Page (ASP). Microsoft-branded, dynamically created Web pages that utilize ActiveX scripting. (Vanguard)

Active X. Software component technologies developed by Microsoft. Although these technologies can be used in any application, they are frequently associated with Internet capabilities. (Vanguard)

Active X Controls. Microsoft-branded software components that allow a user to interact with an application. Examples include entering data, making selections or displaying information. Most commonly associated with Web-based applications in the form of downloadable applications similar to Java "applets." Active X Controls are software language-independent. Frequently used languages are Visual Basic, C++ and scripting languages. Used frequently to "Webify" existing client/server applications. (Vanguard)

Activity Codes. See Wrap-Up Codes.

Adherence to Schedule. A general term that refers to how well agents adhere to their schedules. Also known as real-time adherence. The measure is independent of whether the call center actually has the staff necessary to achieve a targeted service level and/or response time; it is simply a comparison of how closely agents adhere to schedules.

Adherence to schedule generally consists of all logged-on time, including the time spent waiting for transactions to arrive. More specifically, adherence consists of time spent in talk time, after-call work, waiting for calls to arrive, and placing necessary outbound calls. Adherence can also incorporate the issue of timing – when a person was available to take calls. This is sometimes called schedule compliance. The idea is to ensure that agents are logged on for the amount of time required, as well as when required. The two terms most often associated with adherence include:

- Availability – The amount of time agents were available.
- Compliance – When they were available to take calls.

Data for adherence to schedule typically comes from the workforce management system and/or ACD reports. Related terms: Occupancy, Real-Time Adherence Software.

Adult Learning. Training, development or educational efforts focused on adults and adult learning styles. Studies have demonstrated that adults learn differently than children or adolescents. For example, in a training environment, adults:

- Want practical application
- Want their real-life experiences to be recognized and valued
- Are continuous learners and prefer to manage their own learning efforts
- Have varied learning styles
- Need to know why they are learning
- Are motivated most strongly by internal pressures (themselves)
- Want content to be immediately usable

Related terms: Learning Organization, Training Strategy.

Adverse Impact. Legal and HR term. When the same standard, applied to all applicants or employees, affects a protected class more negatively. In the United States, adverse impact is legally defined in Title VII of the Civil Rights Act of 1964.

After-Call Work (ACW). Also called wrap-up, post call processing, average work time or not ready. Work that is necessitated by and immediately follows an inbound call. Often includes entering data, filling out forms and making outbound calls necessary to complete the transaction. The agent is unavailable to receive another inbound call while in this mode. Related terms: Average Handling Time, Queue Dynamics, Talk Time.

Age Discrimination in Employment Act (U.S.). Providing similar coverage to Title VII of the Civil Rights Act, the Age Discrimination in Employment Act of 1967 prohibits employers from discriminating against an applicant or employee based on his or her age.

Agent. The person who handles incoming or outgoing contacts. Also referred to as customer service representative (CSR), customer care representative, telephone sales or service representative (TSR), rep, associate, consultant, engineer, operator, technician, account executive, team member, customer service professional, staff member, attendant or specialist.

Agent Features. Features on a system that are designed for agent use. Example features include login and logout, available, not available, after-call work, transaction codes, supervisor assistance request, call trace indicator (for malicious calls), queue status, audio trouble indication and others. (Vanguard)

Agent Group. Also called split, gate, queue or skills group. An agent group shares a common set of skills and knowledge, handles a specified mix of contacts (e.g., service, sales, billing or technical support) and can be comprised of hundreds of agents across multiple sites. Supervisory groups and teams are often subsets of agent groups.

Mathematically, larger groups of pooled agents are more efficient than smaller groups, at the same service level. All other things equal, if you take several small, specialized agent groups, effectively cross-train them and put them into a single group, the result will be a more efficient environment.

A clear trend in recent years, though, is the recognition that different types of callers often have different needs and expectations, and that different agents with a mix of aptitudes and skills are required to provide the necessary knowledge base. There is a continuum between pooling and specialization, and there is no ideal formula for deciding how pooled or specialized agent groups should be.

However, the symptoms of groups that are too pooled or too specialized are usually evident. For example, symptoms of agent groups that are too specialized include:

- Small groups with low occupancy and/or erratic service level/response time results
- A planning process that is overly complicated
- Many calls are not handled by the intended group (due to overflow)
- Agents become frustrated with narrow responsibilities

Conversely, symptoms of agent groups that are too generalized include:

- Calls have a higher average handling time than necessary, as agents grapple with a broad range of issues
- There is a high number of transferred calls
- Training time is long
- Quality often suffers
- Agents are frustrated with too much to know

In short, agent groups are the building blocks of call center structure. They must reflect – as necessary – product and service requirements, customer requirements, existing skill sets, experience levels and languages. Related terms: Cross-Train, Pooling Principle, Queue Dynamics, Skills-Based Routing.

Agent Occupancy. See Occupancy.

Agent Out Call. An outbound call placed by an agent.

Agent Performance Report. An ACD report that provides statistics for individual agents (e.g., on talk time, after-call work and unavailable time).

Agent Selection. A function in routing software that selects the best agent to handle a call when there is no queue. See Call Selection. (Vanguard)

Agent Status. The mode an agent is in (e.g., talk time, after-call work, unavailable, etc.). See Work State.

Agent Utilization. See Occupancy.

Agents. See Average Number of Agents.

All Trunks Busy (ATB). When all trunks are busy in a specified trunk group. Generally, ATB reports indicate how many times all trunks were busy (how many times the last trunk available was seized), and how much total time all trunks were busy. What they don't reveal is how many callers got busy signals when all trunks were busy. One tell-tale sign of ATB is call arrival patterns that flatten during peak times. Related Terms: Erlang B, Trunk Load.

Alphanumeric. A set of characters that includes both numbers and letters (e.g., AH45908B).

American Society of Composers, Authors and Publishers (ASCAP). An organization that protects copyrights. Fees must be paid to ASCAP for the rights to play recorded music on hold. See Music on Hold.

American Standard Code for Information Exchange (ASCII). A standard for the exchange of data among communications systems.

Americans with Disabilities Act (U.S.). The Americans with Disabilities Act (ADA) of 1990 forbids employment discrimination against individuals with disabilities who can perform the essential functions of the job with or without reasonable accommodations. The disability must be physical or mental and not due to cultural, economic or environmental conditions.

Amortization. An accounting term that refers to the gradual, planned reduction in value of capital expenditures. (*Barron's*)

Analog. Telephone transmission or switching that is not digital. Signals are analogous to the original signal.

Analytics. A general term for advanced reporting and data analysis. In call centers, a set of products or methods that typically interact with CRM systems and multisource data warehouses to collect, analyze and report on particular customer trends or buying patterns. (Vanguard)

Announcement. A recorded verbal message played to callers. See Delay Announcement.

Annual Operating Budget. See Budget.

Annual Operating Plan. An annual operating plan consists of many of the same components as a strategic business plan, but focuses only on the next year. It is more detailed and tactical in nature. It describes how and when the resources needed to carry out tactics will be deployed. See Strategic Business Plan.

Answer Supervision. The signal sent by the ACD or other device to the local or long-distance carrier to accept a call. This is when billing for either the caller or the call center will begin, if long-distance charges apply.

Answered Call. When referring to an agent group, a call is counted as answered when it reaches an agent. Related terms: Handled Call, Offered Call, Received Call.

Application-Based Routing and Reporting. An ACD capability that enables the system to route and track transactions by type of call, or application (e.g., sales, service, etc.) versus the traditional method of routing and tracking by trunk group and agent group.

Application Service Provider (ASP). An outsourcing business that hosts software applications at its own facilities. Customers "rent" the applications, usually for a monthly fee. Applications are usually accessed via the Internet. (Vanguard)

Applications Programming Interface (API). A defined set of programming commands that specify a set of actions that can be initiated by a program or application. It allows an application developer access to the capabilities of a specific system without having to understand the details of how it functions. For example, CTI vendors provide APIs so that third-party applications can perform additional call control functions. (Vanguard)

Architecture. The basic design of a system. Determines how the components work together, system capacity, ability to upgrade and the ability to integrate with other systems.

Area Code. The three-digit number designating a toll center in North America, under the North American Numbering Plan (NANP).

Asset. Anything that an organization owns that has economic value (e.g., cash, real estate, inventory, technology).

Asynchronous Transfer Mode (ATM). A layer 2 WAN and LAN protocol for both real-time and non-real-time applications. ATM has built-in Quality of Service to enable converged network applications of voice, video and data. For call centers, it can be used with TCP/IP to enable VoIP. (Vanguard)

Attempted Call. An outbound term that refers to a call that was made, regardless of results.

Attendant. A person who works at a company switchboard, often called a receptionist or operator. Operator is an alternative term for agent in some call centers, particularly in Europe. See Agent.

Audio Response Unit (ARU). See Interactive Voice Response.

Audiotex. A voice processing capability that enables callers to automatically access pre-recorded announcements. Related terms: Interactive Voice Response, Voice Processing.

Authoritarian Management Style. Managers with authoritarian styles expect their subordinates to carry out orders similar to a chain-of-command environment. The subordinates are not expected to make decisions, so they bear little responsibility for what they are doing. Decision-making takes less time in authoritarian style management, but it may be very difficult to maintain a motivated workforce. Without the ability to contribute to the decision-making process, most employees will feel devalued and resentful. Related term: Participative Management Style.

Auto Available. An ACD feature whereby the ACD is programmed to automatically put agents into available after they finish talk time and disconnect calls. If they need to go into after-call work, they have to manually put themselves there. Related terms: Auto Wrap-Up, Manual Available.

Auto Wrap-Up. An ACD feature whereby the ACD is programmed to automatically put agents into after-call work after they finish talk time and disconnect calls. When they have completed any after-call work required, they put themselves back into available. See Auto Available.

Automated Attendant. A voice processing capability that automates the attendant (operator or receptionist) function. The system prompts callers to respond to choices (e.g., press one for this, two for that...) and then coordinates with the ACD to send callers to specific destinations. This function can reside in an on-site system or in the network. See Interactive Voice Response.

Automated Fulfillment Applications. Applications and/or devices that automate the fulfillment process of traditional customer correspondence, such as letters and faxes. Automating these processes not only enables agents to tackle fulfillment tasks much more quickly, it equips them to track such contacts and tie them to particular customer accounts more easily. Among the features that are included in desktop fulfillment applications are fax server access, automated form/letter generation and text templates for common requests/inquiries, as well as more customer-specific scripting triggered by business rules. See Business Rules.

Automated Greeting. An agent's pre-recorded greeting that plays automatically when a call arrives at his or her telephone station.

Automated Reply. A system-generated email that is automatically sent to a customer acknowledging that his or her email was received. Many automated replies also inform the customer of when to expect a response. See Response Time.

Automatic Answer. See Call Forcing.

Automatic Call Distributor (ACD). The specialized telephone system – or more specifically, a software application – that is used in incoming call centers. Basic ACD capabilities include:

- Route calls: Usually based on the trunk group of the call or the number the caller dialed and routed to the longest available agent in a group. ACDs can also route based on conditional parameters or agent skills.
- Sequence calls: Usually on a first-in/first-out basis. However, ACDs may also change sequence based on information gathered about the call or caller (e.g., from the number dialed or account information in the database).
- Queue calls: When there is no agent available, calls are queued.
- Encourage callers to wait: By playing delay announcements and, in some cases, predicting and announcing wait times.
- Distribute calls among agents: To balance workload as desired and give all agents a chance to excel.
- Capture planning and performance data, both real-time and historical: Most ACDs provide reporting capabilities as a part of the ACD software or as an add-on package.
- Integrate with other systems: The ACD has become just one of many systems in a comprehensive solution.

There are many types of ACDs, including:

- PBX-based ACD (the ACD is a function on a PBX system)
- Standalone ACD (ACD is the sole function)
- Hybrid ACD (via CTI or an add-on server)
- Key Systems
- Centrex (Central Office-based ACD)
- Third Party Managed/Hosted ACD Services

- IP Telephony (IP infrastructure with ACD functionality)

ACD applications have been around since the early 1970s. Since that time, the ACD has been the central nervous system of the call center, making most of the call-routing and call-handling decisions – and having the most information on transactions. Today, the ACD is only one of many technological components that are part of an overall call center solution. As systems are integrated, a variety of databases, Web-based services and other systems are playing a more active role in identifying, routing and handling contacts, and capturing information on these contacts. Related terms: Agent Group, Conditional Routing, Pooling Principle, Skills-Based Routing.

Automatic Call Sequencer (ACS). A simple system that is less sophisticated than an ACD, but provides some ACD-like functionality. See Automatic Call Distributor.

Automatic Number Identification (ANI). A telephone network feature that passes the number of the phone the caller is using to the call center in real-time. ANI may arrive over the D channel of an ISDN PRI circuit (out-of-band signaling) or before the first ring on a single line (in-band signaling). ANI is delivered from long-distance companies. Caller ID is the local phone company version of ANI, and is delivered in-band. ANI is an American term; Calling Line Identity (CLI) is an alternative term used elsewhere. Related terms: Computer Telephony Integration, Dialed Number Identification Service.

Automatic Route Selection (ARS). A feature that enables a telephone system to select the most desirable circuits (e.g., the lowest-cost circuits available) to complete calls.

Automatic Speech Recognition (ASR). See Speech Recognition.

Auxiliary Reason Code. An Avaya term referring to codes entered in the phone by agents to identify the types of activities they are involved in while in an auxiliary work state. See Auxiliary Work State.

Auxiliary Work State. An agent work state that is typically not associated with handling telephone calls. When agents are in an auxiliary mode, they will not receive inbound calls.

Availability. The time agents spend handling calls or waiting for calls to arrive. See Adherence to Schedule.

Available State. The work state of agents who are signed on to the ACD and are waiting for calls to arrive. See Occupancy.

Available Time. The total time that an agent or agent group wait for calls to arrive, for a given time period.

Average Call Value. A measure common in revenue-producing call centers. It is total revenue divided by total number of calls for a given period of time.

Revenue information requires data from several reports/sources (e.g., sales reports, total orders or CRM system reports). In other words, any report that indicates revenue generated by the call center. Total number of calls requires data from ACD reports, and potentially other systems that track contacts (e.g., the ERMS, fax servers and Web servers).

At a basic level, average call value can be used effectively as a KPI to put the value of a revenue-generating call center on a unit basis. However, any metric based on volume of calls, rather than the workload required to handle the calls, presents a trade-off between ease of understanding and depth of understanding. Changes in average talk time or average after-call work affect call center costs, but will not be reflected in an average call value calculation.

An alternative is to measure average value per minute of handle time:

Total revenue ÷ [number of calls x (average talk time + average after-call work)]

Variations on the average call value calculation may be applicable in different call centers, depending on the data available. For example, average call value could be calculated for new customers separately from repeat customers, or for customers of different product lines. Average call value is tough to apply (and generally not recommended) in call centers where the value of calls is difficult to measure (i.e., customer service centers and help desks). Related terms: Incremental Revenue Analysis, Revenue.

Average Delay. See Average Speed of Answer.

Average Delay of Delayed Calls. See Average Time to Abandonment.

Average Delay to Abandon. See Average Time to Abandonment.

Average Handling Time (AHT). The sum of average talk time plus average after-call work. Data on AHT is available from ACD reports for incoming calls, and from ERMS and Web servers for email and Web contacts. AHT may also be available from a workforce management system. AHT is appropriate for high-level purposes and for ongoing tactical planning; it is generally not recommended as a strict agent standard.

In many centers, AHT is increasing as more routine calls are increasingly handled by self-service systems, as contacts requiring agents become more complex, and as objectives focus on building relationships and capturing needed and useful information. However, all things equal, reductions in AHT through better processes, technologies and training will create significant efficiencies. Creating strict AHT targets at the individual level often backfires, resulting in repeat calls, lower quality or in agents using work modes incorrectly (which skews reports). Related terms: Talk Time, After-Call Work.

Average Holding Time on Trunks (AHT). The average time inbound transactions occupy the trunks. It is:

(Talk time + delay time)/calls received

Related terms: Erlang B, Trunk Load.

Average Number of Agents. The average number of agents logged into an ACD group for a specified time period.

Average Speed of Answer (ASA). A measure that reflects the average delay of all calls, including those that receive an immediate answer. It is available from the ACD. Also called average delay.

Average speed of answer is calculated by taking the total time all answered calls have waited and dividing it by the number of answered calls. ASA is typically calculated over a specific timeframe, such as half-hour. Since it is an average, it becomes less meaningful over longer timeframes, such as ASA for the whole day.

The timing of ASA by the ACD generally should begin as soon as the call has queued and is waiting to be answered. With some ACD systems, a message may be played prior to queuing the call, but this time should not be part of the ASA measurement. If your ACD is using overflow, the ASA should reflect the caller's point of view; that is, timing should begin as soon as the call has queued, not at the time the call overflowed.

Some call centers set targets for both ASA and service level. However, for a given service level objective, ASA "will be what it will be" because it comes from the same set of data as service level. In short, it is generally not practical to have objectives for both service level and ASA. (However, ASA can be a viable substitute if service level is so low that few or no calls are registering in the service level measure.)

(continued, next page)

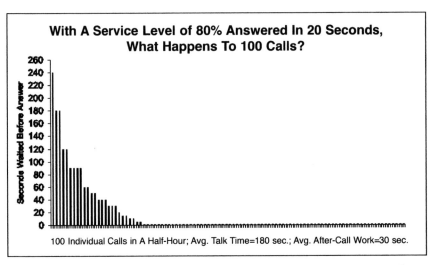

With A Service Level of 80% Answered In 20 Seconds, What Happens To 100 Calls?

Seconds Waited Before Answer

100 Individual Calls in A Half-Hour; Avg. Talk Time=180 sec.; Avg. After-Call Work=30 sec.

It is also important to remember that ASA does not reflect a "typical caller's experience." Most calls get answered more quickly than ASA, and some wait far beyond ASA (see illustration). Related terms: Average Delay of Delayed Calls, Queue Dynamics, Service Level.

Average Time to Abandonment (ATA). Also called average delay to abandon. The average time that callers wait in queue before abandoning. The calculation considers only the calls that abandon. Related term: Caller Tolerance.

Average Work Time (AWT). See After-Call Work.

Back Office. Business applications and functions that are "behind the scenes" to a customer. Examples include accounting, finance, inventory control, fulfillment, productions and human resources. Back-office applications are often associated with enterprise resource planning systems. Related terms: Enterprise Resource Planning, Front Office.

Backbone. The part of the communications network that carries the most traffic (e.g., the services that connect cities, LANs or call centers).

Balance Sheet. A balance sheet displays the assets of an organization, its liabilities, capital and equity. It shows the difference between assets and liabilities, which is the organization's equity, or net worth. This provides six types of information regarding the organization:

- Information on how capital is invested and how the capital structure is divided between senior issues and common stock
- Strength or weakness of the working-capital position
- Reconciliation of the earnings reported in the income account
- Data to test the true success or prosperity of the business, the amount earned on invested capital
- The basis for analyzing the sources of income
- The basis for a long-term study of the relationship between earning power and asset values and of the development of the financial structure

Related terms: Cash-Flow Statement, Income Statement, Statement of Retained Earnings.

Balanced Scorecard. A management methodology/approach attributed to Robert S. Kaplan and David P. Norton that supplements traditional financial measures with criteria that measures performance from three additional perspectives – those of the customer, internal business processes, and learning and growth. It is designed to enable companies to track financial results while simultaneously monitoring progress in building the capabilities and acquiring the intangible assets they need for future growth.

Bandwidth. The transmission capacity of a communications line.

Barge-In. An ACD feature that allows a supervisor or manager to join or "barge-in" on a call being handled by an employee.

Base Pay. The fixed pay an employee receives on a regular basis for work performed.

B

Base Staff. Also called seated agents. The minimum number of agents required to achieve service level and response time objectives for a given period of time. Seated agent calculations assume that agents will be "in their seats" for the entire period of time. Therefore, schedules need to add in extra people to accommodate breaks, absenteeism and other factors that will keep agents from the phones. Related term: Rostered Staff Factor.

Baseline Survey. A survey conducted for the purpose of providing a baseline measure or benchmark that can be used as a comparison point going forward.

Basic Rate Interface (BRI). One of two basic levels of ISDN service. A BRI line provides two bearer channels for voice and data and one channel for signaling (commonly expressed as 2B+D). Related terms: Integrated Services Digital Network, Primary Rate Interface.

Battery Backup. A support system that provides power to telecommunications or data systems should a power outage occur.

Beep Tone. An audible notification that a call has arrived. Beep tone can also refer to the audible notification that a call is being monitored. Also called zip tone. Related terms: Automated Greeting, Call Forcing.

Bell Operating Company (BOC). See Regional Bell Operating Company.

Benchmarking. Historically, a term referred to as a standardized task to test the capabilities of devices against each other. In quality terms, benchmarking is comparing products, services and processes with those of other organizations to identify new ideas and improvement opportunities.

Keep some things in mind when considering a benchmarking project and approach. Organizations are different, even within a given industry, so universally accepted standards usually are not defensible. Things like labor rates, caller demographics, caller tolerances, trunk and network configuration, hours of operation and the mix of part-timers and full-timers vary widely. Further, organizations often interpret performance measures differently. For example, one may measure service level as a daily average, another as a monthly average, and another as the number of half-hours per day that met the objective within a specified range.

These cautions in mind, a disciplined, focused benchmarking effort can produce the comparative information necessary to make significant improvements in areas such as forecasting, handling time, first-call resolution and customer satisfaction. See Best in Class.

Best in Class (BIC). A benchmarking term to identify organizations that outperform all others in a specified category. See Benchmarking.

Billing Increment. The unit of time a telecommunications company uses for billing service (e.g., six seconds or 1/10th of a minute).

Binary. A number system based on 1s and 0s. See Digital.

Binaural Headset. A headset with two earpieces, one for each ear. See Headset.

Blended Agent. An agent who handles both inbound and outbound calls, or handles contacts from different channels (e.g., email and phone). See Call Blending.

Blockage. Callers blocked from entering a queue. See Blocked Call.

Blocked Call. A call that cannot be connected immediately because: A) no circuit is available at the time the call arrives, or B) the ACD is programmed to block calls from entering the queue when the queue backs up beyond a defined threshold. Consequently, data on blocked calls may come from your ACD, local telephone company or long-distance provider. When a call is blocked, the caller hears a busy signal. See Controlled Busies.

Bonus. A sum of money given to an employee that is in addition to and separate from base pay. See Base Pay.

Boom. The long, thin part of the headset that holds the microphone at the correct position. See Headset.

Brainstorming. An approach to team decision-making in which members contribute ideas in a free-flowing discussion. It is often used to generate ideas that might otherwise be censored as unrealistic or outside of current conventions.

Branch Office. Typically, a smaller regional or satellite office of a larger company. (Vanguard)

Budget. A summary of proposed or agreed-upon expenditures for a given period of time, for specified purposes. It should outline how the call center will acquire and use resources, and describe how those resources will be deployed and monitored. Effective operating budgets place accountability for the budget on those individuals who have the control to influence call center expenditures.

An operating budget should only include operating expenses, not capital expenditures. An annual operating budget covers a one-year period of time, and ensures that an organization will have the amount of funding necessary to meet objectives, while also ensuring that the organization does not overspend to meet these goals. See Variance Reports.

Bureaucratic Organizational Design. See Organizational Design.

Business Environment. The environment in which organizations operate. It consists of external factors that can be divided into two broad categories:

- The market environment: The market environment is comprised of the factors that create what Adam Smith called the "invisible hand." Components of the market environment include revenue, profits, production, finance, market strategy, competitors – in short, those things that are part of supply and demand. These forces are regulated by competition, choice and consumer behavior and should drive the organization's competitive strategy.

- The nonmarket environment: The nonmarket environment is characterized by political, legal and social arrangements outside of market forces. Components of the nonmarket environment include regulation, health and safety issues, trade policy, legislation, politics, the media and public pressures. These forces are intermediated by public and private institutions (e.g., regulators, courts, legislatures and public consensus).

The nonmarket environment shapes business opportunities in the market environment. For example, regulatory policies on privacy impact customer communication strategies and how firms can compete to win and serve customers. Similarly, market issues can impact the nonmarket environment (e.g., consumers who were unable to easily obtain their own credit reports demanded regulations that stipulate minimum customer access requirements for credit reporting bureaus). See Strategy.

Business Relationship Management (BRM). See Customer Relationship Management.

Business Rules. A phrase used to refer to various software (or manual) controls that manage contact routing, handling and follow up. Often used interchangeably with workflow. When you go to your favorite Web site and the screen greets you by name, a business rule that checked for a cookie on your computer correctly presented the personalized greeting. When you call your bank and the IVR selection you choose most frequently is presented as the first option, a sophisticated business rule has learned from your past interactions.

Viewed simplistically, business rules are nothing but a sequence of "if-then" statements. But when the entire range of possible actions that can be undertaken by an organization is represented by such simple statements, the result can be a dense and complex forest of decision trees. Computer software and hardware can negotiate the complexity – that's rarely the problem – but human beings have to develop the business rules. See Customer Relationship Management.

Business to Business (B-to-B). Refers to business or interactions between businesses. See Business to Consumer.

Business to Consumer (B-to-C). Refers to business or interactions between a business and consumers. See Business to Business.

Busy. In use, or "off hook."

Busy Hour. A telephone traffic engineering term, referring to the hour of time in which a trunk group carries the most traffic during the day. The average busy hour reflects the average over a period of days, such as two weeks. Busy hour has little use for incoming call centers, which require more specific resource calculation methodologies.

Busy Season. The busiest time of a year for a call center. For example, many catalog companies have a busy season in the months that lead up to Christmas.

C-Level. A reference to top management in an organization, specifically to executives whose titles include CEO, CIO, CFO, CCO and others. (This term is attributed to industry analyst Paul Anderson.)

Cable Modem. A device that provides high-speed Internet access over cable TV infrastructure. It is used for, but not limited to, application system access and VoIP for work-at-home (telecommuting) agents. (Vanguard)

Calibration. In a call center, calibration is the process in which variations in the way performance criteria are interpreted from person to person are minimized. In a typical calibration session, the people who routinely monitor agents individually monitor the same call. The ratings and/or scores are then discussed until the group comes to consensus on the most appropriate ratings and/or scores. The calibration component of a monitoring program is crucial because it provides consistency, reduces the likelihood of agents questioning fairness and continuously develops and assesses monitoring criteria.

Calibration is not a quick or easy process; it takes a considerable commitment. Initially, it may take many hours of discussion and practice before a team begins to score a call the same way. Calibration should be an ongoing activity. See Monitoring.

Call. Also called contact or transaction. Although it most often refers to a telephone call, call can also refer to a video call, a Web call and other types of customer contacts. In a broader sense, call literally means "to visit." See Call Center.

Call Blending. Traditionally, the ability to dynamically allocate call center agents to both inbound and outbound calling based on conditions in the call center and programmed parameters. This enables a single agent to handle both inbound and outbound calls from the same position without manually monitoring call activity and reassigning the position. The outbound dialing application monitors inbound calling activity and assigns outbound agents to handle inbound calls as inbound volume increases, and assigns inbound agents to outbound calling when the inbound volume drops off. More recently, call blending has evolved to also refer to blending calls with non-phone work or handling contacts from different channels (e.g., email and phone). See Blended Agent.

Call-by-Call Routing. The process of routing each call to the optimum destination according to real-time conditions. Related terms: Network, Network Interflow, Percent Allocation.

Call Center. ICMI defines call center as: "A coordinated system of people, processes, technologies and strategies that provides access to organizational resources through appropriate channels of communication to enable interactions that create value for the customer and organization."

Essentially, call center has evolved into an umbrella term that generally refers to groups of agents handling reservations, help desks, order functions, information lines or customer services, regardless of how they are organized or what types of transactions they handle. Characteristics of a call center generally include:

- Calls (contacts) go to a group of people, not a specific person. In other words, agents are cross-trained to handle a variety of contacts.
- Routing and distribution systems (e.g., ACD systems and/or email response management systems) are generally used to route distribute contacts among agents, put calls in queue when all agents are occupied and provide essential management reports.
- Call centers often use advanced network services (e.g., 800 service, DNIS, ANI) and many use interactive voice response capabilities.
- Agents have real-time access to current information via specialized database programs (e.g., status of customer accounts, products, services and other information).
- Management challenges include forecasting calls, calculating staffing requirements, organizing sensible schedules, managing the environment in real-time and *getting the right people in the right places at the right times, doing the right things.*

As organizations everywhere transition telephone-centric centers into multichannel environments, many are questioning the term call center. Examples of alternative terms include:

- Contact center
- Interaction center
- Customer care center
- Customer support center
- Customer communications center
- Customer services center
- Sales and service center
- Technical support center
- Help desk

Additionally, industry-related terms, such as reservations center (the travel industry), hotline (emergency services) and trading desk (financial services), are commonly found in specific types of organizations.

It's interesting to note that "call" literally means "visit." It is a term that's been around many centuries, and we're calling on each other today via email, chat, video, the Web and, of course, telephone. "Center," on the other hand, is more problematic in literal meaning, given the many multisite configurations. Just remember:

- When people use the term call center, they are often referring to the same environments others think of as contact or interaction centers.

- When people use the term contact center, they are not necessarily referring to an environment that handles a broader variety of contact channels than other typical call centers.

- The vast majority of centers are handling more than telephone calls, and have for some time.

- Contact centers, help desks, reservations centers, emergency services centers, information lines and the like *are* call centers, assuming a broad interpretation of the term.

The jury is still out on the terms, and which will emerge as front-runners in coming years. In the mean time, we need to be able to explain to people outside the industry that all of these terms are referring to a very unique environment that is customer demand-driven, has unique management requirements, and is essential in a real-time, communications-driven economy. (Note, this dictionary uses the term call center to refer to any customer contact/customer interaction environment.) See Call Center Value Proposition.

Call Center Initiated Assistance. Typically, this refers to a text-chat session initiated by the agent, rather than the customer.

Call Center Management. ICMI defines call center management as: "The art of having the right number of skilled people and supporting resources in place at the right times to handle an accurately forecasted workload, at service level and with quality."

This definition can be boiled down to two major objectives: 1) Get the right people and supporting resources in the right places at the right times, and 2) do the right things. In other words, provide accessibility with quality. These themes run throughout call center management, from strategic decisions down to day-to-day tactics. See Call Center.

Call Center Value Proposition. The set of benefits that the call center provides to the organization. Defining the call center's value proposition has wide-reaching implications. Organizational perception of call center value affects budget allocations, strategic objectives and direction, technology resources, management authority and autonomy, levels of interdepartmental cooperation and even the quality and commitment of personnel assigned to the call center.

The following are generally recognized areas in which call centers add strategic value:

- Business unit strategies: With advanced data warehousing and mining capabilities available today, call centers are collecting and analyzing more and more information for other business units, enabling them to make better strategic and operational decisions.

- Customer satisfaction and loyalty: Building customer relationships that enable customer satisfaction and encourage loyalty has become a strategic necessity for organizations today. As most organizations' primary customer touch point, the call center is key in achieving these objectives.

- Quality and innovation: Many organizations today must differentiate themselves among many competitors and alternative services. Call centers provide the organization with customer data to make innovative improvements that will meet the needs of their most valuable customers.

- Marketing: In addition to its traditional role of supplying marketing with response rate data and feedback, today's call center also carries out marketing strategies (e.g., customer profiling and segmentation).

- Products and services: As customer segmentation becomes more advanced in organizations today, the call center provides insight from the customer into which products and services will best meet the needs of each customer segment.

- Efficient service delivery: Increasing operational efficiency has long been a primary goal of organizations. However, as customers continue to demand more access alternatives and expanded service availability, the call center becomes that much more vital to the organization's ability to service them effectively and efficiently.

- Self-service usage and system design: With the growth of ecommerce, customers are demanding greater levels of self-service. Call centers provide both the data for determining the best way to offer those services, as well as personal support when self-service options become insufficient.

- Revenue/sales: For-profit organizations continue to seek ways to increase wallet share of customers. Call centers assist with that objective by providing well-trained agents who have the tools to upsell and cross-sell effectively.

Call center managers need to be aware of all the benefits a call center can provide, and then they need to establish which sets of benefits best fit their call center's role in their organization. This is a dynamic, ongoing process. See Call Center.

Call Control Variables. The set of criteria the ACD uses to process calls. Examples include routing criteria, overflow parameters, recorded announcements and timing thresholds.

Call Detail Recording (CDR). A telephone system feature that allows the system to record the details of incoming and outgoing calls (e.g., when they occur, how long they last and which extensions they go to). Also called station message detail recording.

Call Forcing. An ACD feature that automatically delivers calls to agents who are available and ready to take calls. They hear a notification that the call has arrived (e.g., a beep tone), but do not have to press a button to answer the call. Sometimes called automatic answer. See Manual Answer.

Call Load. Also called workload. Call load is volume multiplied by average handling time, for a given period of time. Although the process of forecasting may initially project volume and average handling time separately, the forecast must ultimately bring these components together into an overall forecast of call load.

Call Management System (CMS). Another term for an ACD reporting system.

Call Mix. A generic term that describes the mix of call types (e.g., 50 percent sales calls and 50 percent technical support calls).

Call Quality (Contact Quality). Typically, a measure that assigns a value to the quality of individual contacts. Call quality is a common and appropriate measure in all environments as both a high-level objective (overall summary of the results of individual contacts), which is generally tracked monthly, and as the basis for specific objectives for agents and supervisors, contact by contact.

The quality of each contact is essential to successful call center performance. Quality should be defined to reflect the needs and objectives of both the organization and customers. Criteria generally include such things as interpreting customer requirements correctly, entering data accurately, providing the correct information, accurate call coding, and capturing needed and useful information.

The criteria that applies to agents should be an inherent part of monitoring and coaching processes. Data typically comes from samples via monitoring and/or recording contacts; however, some criteria may also be generated from ACD-based call coding or reports from customer information systems.

It's important to note that, in addition to those criteria that define a quality call on an individual basis, a much larger set of issues should be explored. The following are components of a quality call when viewed at an organizationwide level:

- Customer does not get a busy signal when using telephone or "no response" from Web site
- Customer is not placed in queue for too long
- Agent provides correct response
- All data entry is correct
- Agent captures all needed/useful information
- Agent has "pride in workmanship"
- Contact is necessary in the first place
- Customer receives correct information
- Customer has confidence contact was effective
- Customer doesn't feel it necessary to check-up, verify or repeat
- People "down the line" can correctly interpret the order
- Customer is not transferred around
- Customer doesn't get rushed
- Customer is satisfied
- Unsolicited marketplace feedback is detected and documented
- Call center's mission is accomplished

From this broad perspective, defining, assessing and improving quality becomes an organizationwide effort. Related terms: Monitoring, System of Causes.

Call Recording. A type of monitoring in which the supervisor or automated system records a sampling of calls. The person conducting the monitoring then randomly selects calls for evaluation of agent performance. See Quality Monitoring System.

Call Selection. A function in routing software that selects the best call for an agent to handle when there is a queue and an agent has come available. See Agent Selection. (Vanguard)

Call Taping. See Call Recording.

Call Treatment. A term that refers generally to announcements, music, busy signals, ringing or recorded information provided to callers while they are in queue. (Vanguard)

Callback Information Capture. Gathering information about a caller to be used in callbacks. Passive capture is done without the caller's knowledge; for example, capturing ANI from abandoned calls. Active capture requests the caller to enter callback information through a voice response system, switch prompting, interactive Web page or voicemail message. Callbacks are then logged and delivered to agents, either through automatically queuing the callbacks to available agents or by providing the callback messages to agents for them to dial. (Vanguard)

Callback Messaging. A feature that enables callers waiting in queue to leave a message or to enter their telephone numbers for later callback from an agent.

Caller Entered Digits (CED). The digits a caller enters on his or her telephone keypad. Usually used for auto attendant, voice response and CTI applications. Also referred to as prompted digits.

Caller ID. See Automatic Number Identification.

Caller Tolerance. How patient callers will be when they encounter queues or busy signals. There are seven factors of caller tolerance, which include:

1. Degree of motivation: How motivated are callers? For example, those experiencing a power outage will usually wait longer to reach their utility than catalog customers placing an order for merchandise.

2. Availability of substitutes: Are there substitutes callers can use (e.g., Web or IVR services) if they can't get through to the initial number? If they are highly motivated and have no substitutes, they will retry many times if they get busies and generally will wait a long time in queue, if necessary.

3. Competition's service level: If it's easier for callers to use competitive services, they may go elsewhere.

4. Level of expectations: An organization or industry's reputation for service – or the level of service being promoted – has a bearing on caller tolerance.

5. Time available: The time callers have when attempting to reach the center can have a large impact on tolerance. For example, doctors who call insurance providers are infamous for being intolerant of

even modest queues; retirees, on the other hand, may be more forgiving.

6. Who's paying for the call: In general, callers are more tolerant of a queue when toll-free service is available. They are less tolerant of a queue when they are paying toll charges.

7. Human behavior: The weather, the caller's mood, the time of day and other human behavior factors all have a bearing on caller tolerance.

These factors influence such things as how long callers will wait in queue, how many callers will abandon, how many will retry when they get busy signals, how they will react to automation, such as IVR or Web services, and how they perceive the service the call center is providing.

The factors that influence tolerance are constantly changing, which makes predicting abandonment difficult. Even so, it is important to have a general understanding of the factors affecting callers' tolerance so that you can better understand caller behavior and establish services that meet your callers' needs and expectations. Related terms: Abandoned Call, Delay Announcements.

Calling Line Identity (CLI). See Automatic Number Identification.

Calls in Queue. A real-time report that refers to the number of calls received by the ACD system but not yet connected to an agent.

Calls Per Agent. See Contacts Handled.

Capital Budgeting. A method for evaluating, comparing and selecting projects to achieve the best long-term financial gain. See Capital Expenditures. (*Barron's*)

Capital Expenditures. Long-term expenditures that are amortized over a period of time, determined by IRS regulations. See Capital Budgeting. (*Barron's*)

Career Path. Career paths guide individual development through structured advancement opportunities within the call center and/or organization. Most career paths require specific tasks to be successfully accomplished in order to move from one level to the next. In most career path programs, base pay increases are dependant on advancement to the next position and variable pay is linked to performance.

A typical career path model requires the development of job families, which are comprised of a number of jobs arranged in a hierarchy by grade, pay and responsibility (e.g., agent, team leader, supervisor, manager, senior manager and director). The career path then indicates the requirements for each job within the family (e.g., education, experience, tenure, knowledge, skills and behavioral competencies). Many organizations also require cross-functional experience to provide a broader, organizational perspective. Generally, this involves a job rotation in other functions, such as marketing, sales or finance.

The basic career path process involves three key phases:

1. Assessment phase: Individual assessment through performance appraisals, coaching/mentoring, skills assessment and interests evaluation, which identifies the strengths and weaknesses of the individual.

2. Direction phase: Direction and goal-setting, in which the employee decides on the type of career he or she wishes to pursue and identifies the necessary steps to attain it.

3. Development phase: Development, which includes taking the necessary steps or actions to increase skills to prepare for promotions, such as job rotation, special projects/assignments, seminars/workshops and self-paced training.

Because the historical corporate-ladder approach to staff development can be limited for call centers (due to the finite amount of supervisory and management positions available), many call centers are focusing instead on creating skill paths for their employees. See Skill Path.

Carrier. A company that provides telecommunications circuits. Carriers include both local telephone companies, also called local exchange carriers (LECs), and long-distance providers, also called inter-exchange carriers (IXCs).

Case-Based Reasoning. Business application that aids in analyzing and resolving problems based on cases that are recorded in the database. New cases are added to the database as additional problems are resolved or resolved in new ways. May be part of a bigger support system known as a knowledge base. See Knowledge Base. (Vanguard)

Cash-Flow Statement. The cash-flow statement details the sources of cash coming into and flowing out of an organization. This statement provides information on the health of an organization's earnings and how they are using cash. An income statement and balance sheet are needed to prepare a cash-flow statement. The activity is divided into three different categories – operating activities, investing activities and financing activities. Related terms: Balance Sheet, Income Statement, Statement of Retained Earnings.

Cause-and-Effect Diagram. A chart that illustrates the relationships between causes and a specific effect you want to study. The traditional cause categories used in these diagrams are often referred to as the "4Ms," manpower, machines, methods and materials. A variation on these categories – people, technology, methods and materials/information – works better for call centers. However, these labels are only suggestions, and you can use any that help your group creatively focus on and think through the problem. Possible causes leading to the effect are drawn as branches off the main category. The final step is to prioritize the causes and work on the most prevalent problems first.

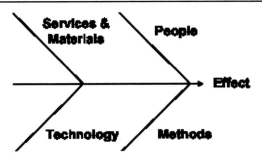

The cause-and-effect diagram illustrates the relationships between causes and a specific effect. Possible causes leading to the effect are drawn as branches off the main category.

Example applications include the study of:
- Long calls
- Repeat calls
- Poor adherence to schedule
- Inaccurate forecast

The cause-and-effect diagram, alternatively called a fishbone diagram because of its shape, was first developed by Dr. Kaoru Ishikawa of the University of Tokyo, in the mid-1900s. It has since become recognized and used worldwide.

Central Office (CO). Can refer to either a telephone company switching center or the type of telephone switch used in a telephone company switching center. The local central office receives calls from within the local area and either routes them locally or passes them to an interexchange carrier (IXC). On the receiving end, the local central office receives calls that originated in other areas from the IXC.

Centrex. A central office telephone switch service that serves a specific area. Similar to a PBX, except that it is owned by the local telephone company and is used by multiple business and/or residential customers. For call centers, it is an alternative to buying, maintaining and administering your own voice switch. (Vanguard)

Centum Call Seconds (CCS). A unit of telephone traffic measurement referring to 100 call seconds. The first C represents the Roman numeral for 100. 1 hour of telephone traffic = 1 Erlang = 60 minutes = 36 CCS. Related terms: Erlang, Erlang B, Erlang C.

Chaos Mentality. A call center workforce management culture that relies on real-time reactions to ongoing changes in queue conditions. A chaos mentality is evident when agents are continually asked to get on and off the phone throughout the day as the queue ebbs and flows. Related term: Planning Culture.

Checklist. A quality tool. Is often a list of process steps (e.g., key procedures).

Chief Information Officer (CIO). A typical title for the highest ranking executive responsible for an organization's information systems.

Circuit. A transmission path between two points in a network.

Circuit Switching. A method of transferring information across a network by establishing a temporary, dedicated, end-to-end path (a circuit) for the duration of a communication. This is the technology traditionally used to transmit voice (e.g., over the public switched telephone network). (Vanguard)

Class of Service (COS). A method of tagging data packets for special handling, usually at a higher priority. For call centers, this technique is used to enable VoIP services. (Vanguard)

Client. Usually refers to the client in a client/server environment. The client is a computer or computer application that has access to services (data, software) over a network from a server application. Related terms: Desktop Technologies, Thin Client, Thick Client. (Vanguard)

Client/Server Architecture. A networked computing approach in which one computer application (client) issues a request to another computer application (server). The server application processes the request and delivers the requested information back to the client application. A computer can be a client in one application process, and a server in another process. Call center client/server applications include but are not limited to CTI, IVR and CRM. Related term: Desktop Technologies. (Vanguard)

Co-Browsing. A term that refers to the capability of both an agent and customer to see a Web page and share navigation and data entry.

Co-Sourcing Arrangement. See Managed Staffing Arrangement.

Coaching. Feedback given during ongoing meetings (formal and/or informal) between an individual and his/her manager to discuss performance, development, career, etc. Coaching can be thought of as one-on-one interactive training.

Coaxial Cable. An insulated, protected wire (the kind used for cable TV) capable of high-speed services.

Collateral Duties. Non-phone tasks (e.g., data entry) that are flexible and can be scheduled for periods when call load is slow. Related terms: Schedule, Schedule Alternatives.

Commissions. Monetary compensation given to agents for meeting or exceeding sales goals. Sales agents may be paid on a straight commission or salary plus commission (although some call centers pay sales agents on a straight salary basis).

Common Carrier. A company that provides communications services to the public.

Common Causes. Causes of variations that are inherent to a process over time. They cause the rhythmic, common variations in the system of causes, and they affect every outcome of the process and everyone working in the process. Related terms: Control Chart, Special Causes.

Common Gateway Interface (CGI). A program running on a Web server that enables dynamic activities on a Web page. (Vanguard)

Common Object Request Broker Architecture (CORBA). A programming standard and framework from the object management group that utilizes object-oriented programming to enable software programs to interoperate. It is programming language independent and utilizes a software device called an object request broker to pass messages between programs. (Vanguard)

Communications Server. An alternative to the PBX that manages and routes voice, fax, Web and email communications within a single server and provides a wide set of applications. Typically based on a Windows NT platform. Communications servers are generally seen in small to medium (fewer than 100 agents) call centers that can benefit from an integrated solution that otherwise would be cost-prohibitive as separate point solutions (e.g., PBX, voicemail, IVR, ACD, CTI, quality monitoring). (Vanguard)

Compact Disc Read-Only Memory (CD-ROM). These computer discs hold as much as 660 megabytes of memory. Information is optically stored and read by laser.

Compensable Factor. Work-related criterion that an organization considers important in assessing the relative value of different jobs.

Compensation. Payment for services provided by employees. An employee's total compensation has three components:

1. Base pay (the fixed amount a person receives; i.e., salary or hourly wages)
2. Incentives (rewards for performance; e.g., bonuses)
3. Benefits

Job-based pay determines compensation according to the value of the job. Skills-based pay places value on an employee's abilities, potential and flexibility to handle multiple job responsibilities or duties. Because of the often limited advancement opportunities in call centers, skills-based pay can be an effective way to provide agents with room to grow professionally. Related terms: Career Path, Skill Path.

Competitive Local Exchange Carrier (CLEC). See Local Exchange Carrier.

Completed Call. A general term that refers to an inbound contact that successfully reaches and is handled by an agent. Can also refer to an outbound call that successfully reaches a live person (or answering machine, if leaving a message is acceptable). In an outbound context, also called connected call.

Compliance. See Adherence to Schedule.

Component Object Model (COM). A Microsoft term describing the base model used for building components in an object-oriented programming language. (Vanguard)

Computer-Based Training (CBT). Training programs delivered through software applications without the need for a facilitator. For example, via CBT programs – which may take the form of CD-ROM-, DVD- or Web-based modules – agents can receive refresher courses and product/service updates without the need of supervisory assistance. Computer-based training applications can be embedded right into the agent's desktop. In addition, with some Web-based CBT applications, managers/supervisors can create customized coaching modules online in a matter of minutes, then send the mini-session directly to individual agents at their workstations. CBT is a form of technology-based training (TBT). Related terms: Technology-Based Training, Training, Training Strategy.

Computer Simulation. A computer-based simulator program that predicts the outcome of various events in the future, given many variables. In call centers, it is most often used to determine staff required to meet service levels and response times in complex routing environments. When there are many variables (i.e., as in a skills-based routing environment), computer simulation is often the only way to reasonably predict the required staff. Related terms: Erlang C, Skills-Based Routing.

Computer Telephony Integration (CTI). Enables integration of previously disparate systems to enhance the customer experience and improve operational efficiencies. CTI integrates the functions of telephone networks, voice switching, data switching, computer applications, databases, voice processing and alternative media. With this comes the ability to exchange commands and messages between systems. This results in the ability to monitor and control calls, events, applications, information and endpoints.

CTI can add or enhance functionality in a number of areas:

- Coordinating voice and data:
  - Screen pops, in which information about the caller, associated database files and the call itself are simultaneously delivered to the agent's desktop.
  - Intelligent transfers that enable the caller to be transferred along with associated data to another agent or queue group.
  - IVR coordination that allows for the customer's voice response transactions and inquiries to be transferred to the agent along with the caller.
- Intelligent routing:
  - Conditional routing, which routes calls based on real-time criteria (e.g., calls in queue, time of day, type of call or agent availability).

- Skills-based routing, which matches a caller's specific needs with an agent who has the skills to handle that call on a real-time basis.
- Multisite routing, which routes calls between multiple call centers based on predefined criteria available from a variety of systems.
- Data-directed routing, which routes calls based on information in databases external to the routing system. It is used for applications such as customer segmentation and prioritization.
- Integrated reporting:
  - Cradle-to-grave, which captures the entire caller experience from their initial call to the IVR until they end the call with the last agent.
  - Call and transaction data, which capture and report customer information along with the computer transactions processed during the interaction.
- Desktop softphone:
  - Telephony features, such as login/logout, workstate changes, hold, transfer, conference and others that can be accessed from a window in the agent's monitor.
  - Statistics on agent, queue and group performance that can be made available in a window on the agent's monitor.
- Outbound dialing:
  - Preview dialing, in which information about the person being called is presented to the agent prior to dialing.
  - Predictive dialing, in which calls made by the system are routed to agents along with customer information.
  - Progressive dialing, in which calls are dialed when an agent is available.
  - Call blending, which is the capability to allocate resources between the inbound and outbound modes.

CTI has such far-reaching potential it's important to note the above are simply examples. The functionality of other systems can be enhanced by CTI implementation, as well. (Vanguard)

Concentrated Shift. A scheduling technique that requires agents to work more hours in a day, but fewer days in a week. "Four-by-10" shifts (four days on for 10 hours each, with three days off) are particularly popular with many agents. An important consideration of concentrated shifts is whether agents can handle the longer hours without losing effectiveness. Related terms: Schedule, Schedule Alternatives.

Conditional Routing. The capability of the ACD to route calls based on real-time criteria (e.g., calls in queue, time of day and type of call). It is based on "if-then" programming statements. For example, "if the number of calls in agent group one exceeds 10 and there are at least two available agents in group two, then route the calls to group two."

Confidence Interval. A variable used in determining survey sample size. It indicates how close the survey results of the sample are to the actual results you would get if you surveyed the entire population. Expressed as a plus or minus deviation. See Confidence Level.

Confidence Level. A variable used in determining survey sample size. It indicates how certain you can be that the actual population falls within the confidence interval. Expressed as a percentage. See Confidence Interval.

Connected Call. See Completed Call.

Contact. See Call.

Contact History. The history of a customer's interactions with an organization, generally recorded and stored in a customer information system.

Contact Management System. Business application that enables and tracks each interaction with the customer. Contact management systems also create databases that enable informed communications with customers, such as database marketing and proactive communications. Includes functions such as contact history database and triggers for follow-up contacts. (Vanguard)

Contact Rate. An outbound term that represents the percentage of attempts that result in a contact (contacts divided by attempts).

Contacts. Outbound term that refers to calls that reached the intended person. See Contacts Per Hour.

Contacts Handled (Calls Per Agent). The number of contacts an agent handles in a given period of time. Contacts handled is not a recommended agent performance objective since many of the variables that impact contacts handled are out of agents' control.

Traditionally, contacts handled (also referred to as calls/contacts per agent or calls/contacts per hour) has been an almost universal productivity measurement. In fact, many call center managers have viewed contacts handled as virtually synonymous with "productivity." Contacts handled has been a widely used benchmark for establishing productivity standards, comparing performance among agents and groups, and assessing the impact of changes and improvements to the call center.

However, as a measure of individual performance, contacts handled is, and always has been, problematic. Many of the variables that impact contacts handled are out of agents' control: call arrival rate, type of calls, knowledge of callers, communication ability of callers, accuracy of the forecast and schedule, adherence to schedule (of others in the group) and absenteeism.

There are also mathematical realities at work that are not within the control of an individual agent. For example, smaller groups are less efficient (have lower occupancy) than larger groups at a given service level. Since the number of calls changes throughout the day, so does average calls per agent for a group or an individual in the group. Related terms: Occupancy, Queue Dynamics, True Calls Per Agent.

Contacts Per Hour. An outbound term that refers to the number of contacts divided by agent hours on the dialer. See Contacts.

Continuous Improvement. The ongoing improvement of processes. See System of Causes.

Contract Workers. In the call center context, contractor workers are usually self-employed individuals who form a direct relationship with the organization for specific projects or predefined periods of time. They may be hired on an hourly, day-to-day or week-to-week basis to handle increased interaction volume, provide technology expertise or other call center functions. This gives the call center staffing flexibility (e.g., for seasonal increases, special programs) without the commitment and cost of hiring these employees on a permanent basis.

Typically contract workers are hired for a finite period of time, though an employment contract can also be open-ended. Since the tax burden is shifted from the organization to the contractor, there are legal guidelines for distinguishing contractors from employees.

Control Chart. A quality tool that provides information on variation in a process. One of the reasons that quality problems in the call center are challenging and often confusing is because they are a part of a complex process, and any process has variation from the ideal.

There are two major types of variation: special causes and common causes. Special causes create erratic, unpredictable variation. For example, unusual calls from unexpected publicity or a computer terminal with intermittent problems are special causes. Common causes are the rhythmic, normal variations in the system. A control chart enables you to bring a process under statistical control by eliminating the chaos of special causes. You can then work on the common causes by improving the system and, thus, the whole process.

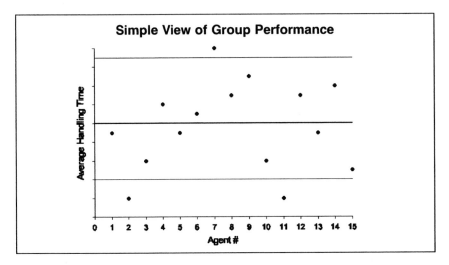

Special causes show up as points outside of the upper control or lower control limits, or as points with unnatural patterns within the limits. A control chart cannot reveal what the problems are. Instead, it reveals where and when special causes occur. Once special causes are eliminated, improving the system itself will have far more impact than focusing on individual causes. Improvements to the system will move the entire process in the "right" direction.

Example applications of the tool include study of:

- Average handling time
- Percent adherence
- Errors and rework
- Requests for supervisory assistance

Related terms: Common Causes, Special Causes, System of Causes.

Controlled Busies. The capability of the ACD to generate busy signals when the queue backs up beyond a programmable threshold. See Blocked Call.

Conventional Shift. A traditional five-day-a-week shift during "normal business hours" (e.g., 9 a.m. to 5 p.m.).

Cookie. A small file in a Web browser that uniquely identifies a user to a Web server to provide personalized content. It is used as an enabling technology in eCRM and Web integration applications. (Vanguard)

Coordinated Voice/Data Conference. A CTI application that provides the ability to conference a data screen along with a voice call, enabling both parties on the conference to view information about the caller. (Vanguard)

Coordinated Voice/Data Consultation. A CTI application similar to coordinated voice/data conference, except that the caller is put on hold while the originally called party consults with a colleague. (Vanguard)

Coordinated Voice/Data Delivery. See Screen Pop.

Coordinated Voice/Data Transfer. A CTI application similar to coordinated voice/data conference, except that the voice call and the data are transferred to a colleague. Often used when transferring a call from an IVR to an agent position with a screen pop. (Vanguard)

Core Values. An organization's core values describe the principles the organization turns to when making its most critical decisions. However, they are not just moral imperatives. They describe simply and concisely how individuals are expected to approach any situation. Some examples of core values include:

- Being a pioneer, not following others
- Encouraging individual ability and creativity
- Attention to consistency and detail
- Opportunity based on merit
- Honesty and integrity
- Excellence in reputation
- Service to the customer above all else

Core values are a key component of branding. A brand publicly describes what an organization says it is, while the values it holds and practices define who the organization actually is. When brand and core values match up and reinforce each other, the organization's image is successfully portrayed. When brand and values conflict, it creates confusion and doubt for employees and customers alike.

Core values, vision and mission are simply three interrelated components of defining and describing an organization's essence. Related terms: Mission, Vision, Strategy.

Cost-Based Pricing. When telecommunications services are priced based upon the cost of providing those services.

Cost/Benefit Analysis. A term used to describe the process of comparing the value of a potential project with the cost associated with it. While different calculations can be used for a cost/benefit analysis, the general concept is to determine if benefits outweigh costs enough to justify implementation.

Cost Center. An accounting term that refers to a department or function in the organization that does not generate profit. When a call center is viewed as a cost center, the focus is on getting the transactions done at the least total cost to the organization. Related term: Profit Center.

Cost of Delay. The direct expense of putting callers in queue. In an inbound call center, each person connected to your system requires a trunk, whether they are talking to an agent or waiting in queue. If you have toll-free service (or any other service that charges a usage fee), you are paying for this time. The cost of delay is expressed in terms of how much you pay for your network service each day for callers to wait in queue until they reach an agent.

Telecommunications costs are inextricably linked to staffing issues. If service level is continually low, the cost of network services will be high. See Queue Dynamics.

Cost Per Call. Total costs (fixed and variable) divided by total calls for a given period of time. There are various ways to calculate cost per call (i.e., determining which factors to include in staff costs, how to allocate equipment, how to value the building), but the basic formula is to divide total costs by total calls received for a given period of time, usually a month. The potential in following cost per call is to identify the variables that are driving it upward or downward, and the impact they have.

A climbing cost per call can be a good sign, depending on the variables driving it up. For example, process improvements may result in fewer calls than would otherwise be necessary (e.g., eliminating the need for customer callbacks, improving the IVR and coordinating with other departments to eliminate problems that generate calls). As a result, the fixed costs (in the numerator) get spread over fewer calls (in the denominator), driving up cost per call. But, of course, total costs will drop over time, because the elimination of waste and rework will drive down variable costs. Similarly, cost per call usually goes down during the busy times of the year, and up during the slower times of year.

Cost per call should be differentiated by each channel of contact.

Figures should also be broken out by types of services provided (i.e., placing orders, changing orders, checking account status, problem resolution, etc.).

Cost Per Contact. See Cost Per Call.

Cost Per Minute. Total expenses divided by agent workload minutes (talk time plus after-call work).

Country Code. The set of digits associated with specific countries that follow the international access code when placing an international call.

Cradle-to-Grave Reporting. A call center reporting term that includes all call center touch points (human and systems) from the time a caller dials an 800 number to the time of disconnect. It can include, but is not limited to, voice-switch routing, IVR, multisite flows, all agent activity and business application activity. The key enabler for cradle-to-grave reporting is typically CTI. (Vanguard)

Critical Path. See Project Management.

Cross-Sell. A suggestive selling technique that offers additional products or services to current customers, usually based on relationships established between the customer's profile and the attributes of customers who have already purchased the products or services being cross-sold.

Cross-Train. To train agents to handle more than one defined mix of calls (e.g., to train technical support agents handling laptop calls to also handle desktop issues).

Cumulative Trauma Disorder (CTD). See Ergonomics.

Customer. Includes individuals, households and/or organizations that have in the past, or may in the future, interact with your organization. Customers may be external (i.e., not a part of your organization) or internal (i.e., members of your organization to which you provide service). See Customer Relationship Management.

Customer Access Strategy. In the call center environment, strategy is embodied in what is often termed a "customer access strategy," which is a framework – a set of standards, guidelines and processes – defining the means by which customers are connected with resources capable of delivering the desired information and services.

As with general corporate strategy, a customer access strategy can take many different forms. However, the most sustainable customer access strategies include the following components:

- Customer segmentation: How customers and the market in general will be segmented and served by the organization. Reflects the organization's cost leadership, differentiation, focus, defender or prospector direction.

- Major contact types: General categories include placing orders, changing orders, checking account status, problem resolution, etc.

- Access channels: The organization's communication channels (e.g., telephone, Web, fax, email, IVR, kiosk, handhelds, face-to-face service and postal mail) along with corresponding telephone numbers, Web URLs, email addresses, fax numbers and postal addresses.

- Service level and response time objectives: How fast the call center intends to respond to customer contacts.

- Hours of operation: The days and hours the call center will be open for business.

- Routing methodology: How, by customer, type of contact and access channel, each contact will be routed and distributed.

- Person/technology resources required: The resources, including people, technologies and databases, required to provide callers with the information and assistance they need, and the organization with the information it needs to track and manage customers and services.

- Knowledge bases: The information systems used to capture, store and process information on customers, products and services.

- Tracking and integration: The methods/systems required to capture information on each customer interaction, and how that data will be used to strengthen customer profiles, identify trends and improve products and services.

While corporate strategy must ultimately define the customer access strategy, the customer access strategy can influence broader corporate strategy. For example, 24x7 call center services have enabled some insurance companies to differentiate their services from competitors who only provide in-person service. Similarly, call center and Web-based sales and services have enabled some computer companies to become low-cost providers vs. competitors who sell through distributors. See Core Values, Mission, Vision, Strategy.

Customer Acquisition. Obtaining new customers. Traditional efforts to attract new customers and grow market share often focus on costly mass-market campaigns, and prices and incentives geared toward "making the sale." In the context of the call center's role in customer relationship management, these objectives are achieved more through positive word-of-mouth and focused efforts to reach specific target markets. See Customer Relationship Management.

Customer Capital. The value of the customer relationships that you have. This includes the depth and quality of those relationships, their ability to generate revenue, how long those relationships last and how profitable they are.

Customer Care. A general term that refers to proactive customer service that creates high levels of customer satisfaction and loyalty. For example, as part of a total customer care program, wireless carriers may call new subscribers, introduce them to the service, go over key features and ensure that customers understand how to contact the company should they have further questions. The term customer care center has become an alternative to call center, particularly in some countries outside of North America. See Call Center.

Customer Care Center. See Customer Care.

Customer Contact. See Call.

Customer Controlled Routing (CCR). A vendor-specific term (originated by Nortel) that refers to a call routing application that enables calls to be handled (e.g., routed, queued, distributed) based on user-defined criteria.

Customer Expectations. The expectations customers have of a product, service or organization. When interacting with organizations, studies have shown that customers have 10 primary expectations, which include (in no specific order):

1. Be accessible
2. Treat me courteously
3. Be responsive to what I need and want
4. Do what I ask promptly
5. Provide well-trained and informed employees
6. Tell me what to expect
7. Meet your commitments; keep your promises
8. Do it right the first time
9. Be socially responsible and ethical
10. Follow up

Related terms: Call Quality, Caller Tolerance, Customer Survey, Customer Relationship Management, Queue Dynamics, Service Level, Response Time.

Customer Information System (CIS). Also called customer interaction software. A database application (or series of integrated applications) that provides information about the customer (e.g., their interactions with the organization, the services and products they have purchased). (Vanguard)

Customer Interaction Management (CIM). See Customer Relationship Management.

Customer Interaction Recording (CIR) System. An application that enables call centers to monitor the performance of both service staff and the center's customer-facing technologies, thus capturing what the customer experiences from the moment they "enter" the call center to the time they "leave."

Customer Interaction Software. See Customer Information System.

Customer Lifetime Value. Expresses the value of a customer to the organization over the entire probable time period that the customer will interact with the organization. Related terms: Customer Loyalty, Customer Relationship Management.

Customer Loyalty. Typically defined in terms of the customer's repurchase behavior, intent to purchase again or intent to recommend the organization. There is usually a link between customer satisfaction and loyalty, with high levels of satisfaction leading to customer loyalty. However, the link is not always clear, and this remains an area of ongoing research. Related terms: Customer Relationship Management, Customer Satisfaction.

Customer-Oriented Organizational Design. See Organizational Design.

Customer Premises Equipment (CPE). A telecommunications term referring to equipment installed on the customer's premises and connected to the telecommunications network.

Customer Profiling. The process of collecting and maintaining information about customers and their relationship to your organization. The information is most often used for customer segmentation and building customer relationships. Customer profiling determines what information about a customer is important to the organization. See Customer Segmentation.

Customer Relationship Management (CRM). The process of holistically developing the customer's relationship with the organization. It takes into account their history as a customer, the depth and breadth of their business with the organization, as well as other factors. Customer relationship management generally uses sophisticated applications and database systems that include elements of data mining, contact management and enterprise resource planning, enabling agents and analysts to know and anticipate customer behavior.

Customer relationship management is both deceptively simple and infinitely complex. The roots of managing customer relationships are as old as human interaction, while the technology used to deploy it is often leading edge. When fully understood and strategically implemented, a renewed focus on the customer relationship can transform an entire organization, as well as vault a beleaguered call center into an unprecedented position of importance.

A common misconception of customer relationship management is that it primarily consists of a database or set of technology tools. Technology is an enabler, but customer relationship management includes much more (e.g., processes, organizational structure, information/data and an understanding of which customers you want to serve and how you will address the needs of different types of customers). Customer relationship management is really about assessing, planning and execution.

There are many terms being used for customer relationship management that can create considerable confusion. CIM (Customer Interaction Management) is preferred by some as more action-oriented. eCRM (electronic CRM) tacks on the lowercase "e" to emphasize the ecommerce aspects involved. eRM (electronic Relationship Management) essentially replaces the customer with the Internet, which may explain why this term has not caught on. ERM (Enterprise Relationship Management) echoes Enterprise Resource Planning (ERP) technology, as does EIM (Enterprise Interaction Management). BRM (Business Relationship Management) distinguishes customers that are actually businesses along the lines of B to B (business-to-business) marketing. There are also other combinations where the lowercase "e" refers to electronic, the uppercase "E" refers to enterprise, the "I" refers to interaction and the "B" refers to business.

Customer relationship management is most clearly understood when broken down into three parts:

- Customer: Customers are, literally, where customer relationship management starts. They include individuals, households and organizations which have interacted with your organization in the past (or may do so in the future). For the purposes of customer relationship management, the term "customer" includes existing and prospective customers, and may also include members of your own organization.

- Relationship: Relationship has several meanings. In one sense, it describes the interactions that an organization has with a customer over time. The relationship consists of a series of contacts between the customer and the organization. In another sense, it refers to the level of loyalty and commitment that the organization and the customer have to each other. The relationship is what sets customer relationship management apart. Much of marketing theory and terminology is adversarial, depicting battlefields upon which the organization will not only tackle competitors, but will seek to capture customers and win market share. Competitors will be outflanked, customers will be targeted, and markets will be dominated. But customer relationship management takes a customer-centric approach that is instantly familiar because it has been so long practiced by successful local proprietors who know and care about their small but loyal customer base.

- Management: Management is the lynchpin of customer relationship management; it embodies the action that must be taken. Customer relationship alone is merely descriptive. What is needed is active, effective management of customer relationships.

Related terms: Business Rules, Customer Loyalty, Customer Satisfaction, Customer Retention Rate.

Customer Retention Rate. The percentage of a prior period's customers who are still customers in the current period (excluding new customers acquired). Customer retention rate results need to be measured against strategic objectives. A related metric would be "saves" or the number of customers whose business was retained after they had indicated their intent to leave. For example, a customer calling to cancel an insurance policy who ends up not canceling it as a result of the agent's efforts on the phone would be a save. Related terms: Customer Loyalty, Customer Relationship Management.

Customer Satisfaction. The level of satisfaction customers have with the organization and the organization's products and services. As an overall measure, customer satisfaction is usually presented as the percentage of all customers who felt satisfied with the service they received.

Studies have linked customer satisfaction to customer loyalty, repeat purchases and word-of-mouth advertising. If customer satisfaction drops, both customers and agents are great sources of information on how to improve results. Customer satisfaction has greatest value as a relative measure and in conjunction with other objectives (e.g., when policies, service level performance, system enhancements and other changes take place, what happens to customer satisfaction?).

There is no standard method for calculating customer satisfaction. The great variety of customers served by different call centers for many different reasons makes it unlikely that there ever will be one standard. However, a variety of industry studies have detailed the behavior of dissatisfied customers. By collecting appropriate data and modeling the impact that changes in the call center could make upon dissatisfied customers, call center managers can cost-justify investments that improve service.

Data for measuring customer satisfaction can come from a variety of sources (e.g., customer satisfaction surveys, mystery shopping, automated IVR surveys and focus groups). Customer satisfaction results are often presented quarterly or monthly, broken down by channel of contact and customer segment. See Customer Loyalty.

Customer Segmentation. The process of grouping customers based on what you know about them, in order to apply differentiated marketing, relationship and contact treatment strategies. A customer segmentation strategy is usually driven by the marketing department, but as the role of call centers grows in importance through the implementation of customer relationship management strategies, call center managers are increasingly recognized as valuable partners in this strategic planning process.

Customer relationship management seeks to segment customers based on their value, or more specifically, their strategic value (not just current profitability). Value segmentation synthesizes knowledge about customers to sort them into actionable groups, based on their importance to the organization. The objective is to allocate the right types and levels of resources to the right customers. Customer strategic value should determine how the relationship with the customer is managed. See Customer Profiling.

Customer Service Representative (CSR). See Agent.

Customer Survey. A process that acquires and assesses feedback from customers or prospective customers. There are four common ways to classify surveys; the specific classification depends on the survey's objectives:

   1. Timeframe/frequency: One-shot surveys, referred to as snapshot,

are intended to measure objectives at a single point in time. Longitudinal surveys gather data over a period of time, usually to detect trends.

2. Breadth of survey: Surveys can either gather data from a cross-section of customers across all segments (or the full range of possible issues across the customer lifecycle) or they can be "pinpoint" surveys that look at only one segment or set of issues.

3. Customer vs. market: Surveys can be conducted with existing customers only or can include a cross-section of the marketplace. A marketplace survey allows for the comparison of your organization's customers with those of other organizations.

4. Customer experience vs. customer expectations: Customer experience surveys are very relevant to customers and usually get a good response rate. Surveys measuring customer expectations, needs and wants usually require incentives unless the respondents are loyal customers who want to tell you what else they want. The problem with customer expectation surveys is that respondents usually say they want everything until faced with the prospect of actually paying for them. Therefore, these survey results are more speculative.

Surveys that are most useful to managers:

- Provide valid information (i.e., representative of the actual body of customers)
- Are simple to implement and administer
- Use an effective rating scale
- Are cheap enough to use at least quarterly, if not monthly
- Allow analysis by type of contact
- Result in reports that are timely, action-oriented and easily understood by call center management and supervisors

Related terms: Confidence Interval, Confidence Level, Customer Loyalty, Customer Satisfaction, Sampling. (TARP)

Customer Valuation Model. A customer valuation model is a mathematical formula that estimates the value of a customer to the organization over a future time period. Value can represent both the tangible and intangible benefits of the customer relationship. The appropriate model to choose for your organization depends on several factors, including strategic objectives, data availability, analytical capability and the nature of your business. A common approach to determine customer valuation is through customer lifetime value. See Customer Lifetime Value.

Cutover. The date and time that a new system is put into use.

Data-Directed Routing. A routing capability that uses a database of information about the customer, current status or other factors to make routing decisions. Generally, it is CTI-enabled. (Vanguard)

Data Mining. The use of analytical tools to uncover correlation between disparate sets of data. With these tools, an analyst can test hypotheses about data (e.g., how many customers who purchased antilock brakes as an option also upgraded their warranty package?), and the mining tool can also derive correlation between hypotheses not yet determined. A mining tool may find that, of customers who purchased antilock brakes and an extended warranty, 85 percent were between the ages of 32 and 45 with an average of 2.4 children. This derived information can be fed into scripts, workflows and marketing campaigns to strengthen relationships and enhance customer value. The ultimate objective is to understand and serve customers better. (Vanguard)

Data Switch. A LAN or WAN networking device that connects a series of computers via high-speed transmission paths. Each computer has its own dedicated bandwidth or segment. (Vanguard)

Data Warehousing. A large database that stores data generated by an organization's multiple business systems. Data can be extracted using report generators, sophisticated decision support systems or other analytical tools. Related term: Data Mining. (Vanguard)

Database. An application that contains data that is organized in a structured fashion for quick access.

Database Call Handling. A CTI application whereby the ACD works in sync with the database computer to process calls based on information in the database. For example, a caller inputs his or her account number or other type of identifier into a voice processing system, the database retrieves information on that customer and then issues instructions to the ACD on how to handle the call (e.g., where to route the call, what priority the call should be given in queue, the announcements to play).

Database Marketing. Using information in a customer database as the basis for a focused marketing campaign.

Datamart. A subset of a data warehouse, typically with data that is of interest to a particular department of an organization. See Data Warehousing. (Vanguard)

Day-of-Week Routing. A network service that routes calls to alternate locations, based on the day of week. There are also options for day-of-year and time-of-day routing.

Dedicated Circuit. A point-to-point telecommunications channel used by a single subscriber or for a single purpose.

Delay. Also called queue time. The time a caller spends in queue waiting for an agent to become available. Average delay is the same thing as average speed of answer. Related terms: Average Delay of Delayed Calls, Average Speed of Answer.

Delay Announcement. A recorded announcement designed and positioned to encourage callers to wait for an agent to become available, have information ready (e.g., their account number, provide information pertaining to the delay, or suggest other access alternatives or times callers can get assistance). In some systems, delay announcements are provided through recorded announcement (RAN) routes.

Most inbound call centers provide delay announcements to callers who wait in queue. An example of an often-used delay announcement is: "All of our representatives are currently assisting other callers. Your call is important to us..." Typically, at least two delay announcements are presented. The first announcement recognizes callers, explains the delay and promises that the calls will be answered. This announcement should also advise them of what to have ready for the call (e.g., account number) and provide alternative contact methods (e.g., "visit our Web site at www...").

The purpose of a second delay announcement is to give callers who are about to abandon renewed assurance that you will get to them: "Thank you for your patience. Please continue to hold and one of representatives will assist you shortly."

There are other variations of delay announcements commonly used in call centers. Examples include:

- Situation-specific messages: Announcements intended to off-load what would otherwise be routine calls. Utilities use messages such as: "We are aware of the power outage in the Southwest area caused by nearby construction. We hope to have power restored by 2 p.m. We apologize for the inconvenience. If you need further assistance, please stay on the line. One of our representatives will be with you momentarily..."

- Redirection messages: Announcements designed to encourage customers to use other channels or numbers. For example, "Thank you for calling Skyway airline. If you would like to use our automated flight arrival and departure system, please press one, or visit our Web site at www..."

Related terms: Abandoned Call, Caller Tolerance, Fast Clear Down, Queue.

Delay Before Answer. See Ring Delay.

Depreciation. According to *Barron's*, depreciation is: "The allocation of an asset's cost, for tax or management purposes, based on its age." The government's tax body (e.g., the IRS in the United States) generally stipulates a certain method (based on the item being purchased) for tax purposes. However, management can choose from several different methods for internal evaluation. The method chosen can have a substantial impact on the purchase decision. Four major methods of depreciation include:

- Modified Accelerated Cost Recovery System (MACRS): The method required by the IRS for property placed in service after 1986. Pronounced "makers."

- Straight-line method: A simple method that assumes an asset is used at a constant rate over its useful life.

- Sum-of-the-years'-digits method: Assumes an asset will be more useful in the earlier part of life. This method gives higher depreciation charges to earlier years of depreciation.

- Double-declining balance method: A method popular before MACRS became mandatory, but not used as much today. It results in depreciation charges that are less than the purchase cost of the asset.

Understanding basic depreciation principles can help managers make better capital budgeting decisions. Related terms: Capital Budgeting, Capital Expenditures.

Desktop Application. Software programs, such as word processors, spreadsheets, database programs, contact management programs and other applications that reside on (or are accessed from) the computer at an individual's PC.

Desktop Softphone. See Softphone.

Desktop Statistics. Real-time and/or historical information on call center activities delivered to desktop PCs. This function enables supervisors to view call center activities and agents to access information on their own activities. (Vanguard)

Desktop Technologies. Generally refers to the range of desktop technologies that are available. Desktop technologies come in many shapes and sizes, each with their own dependencies and advantages. Key terms include:

- Client/Server Architecture: A networking scheme in which a client application requests information from a server application.
- Client: A computer or computer application that has access to services (data, software) over a network from a server application.
- Server: A computer that shares its resources with other computers on a network. For example, file servers share disk storage with other computers. Database servers respond to requests from other computers on the network (clients).
- Fixed-function "dumb" terminal: The user device (terminal) in a computing environment in which all of the processing occurs on a central computer or mainframe.
- PC-running terminal emulation: This duplicates the functionality of the "dumb" terminal in environments that require PCs for some applications, but in which access to a mainframe is still necessary.
- Thick client: A workstation in a client-server environment that performs much or most of the application processing. It requires programs and data to be installed on it and a significant part of the application processing takes place on the workstation. The client is "thick" in that much of the overall application is running on it.
- Thin client: A workstation in a client-server environment that performs little or no application processing. Often used to describe browser-based desktops. The client is "thin" in that the applications reside on and are run within the server rather than the client.

The functionality and speed of the desktop have a significant impact on performance statistics. It is critical that the IT team understands the time-sensitive nature of call centers when configuring applications. (Vanguard)

Desktop Telephony. See Softphone.

Development. Learning focused on long-term growth in the individual's or organization's capabilities and skills. Related terms: Development Plan, Education, Learning, Performance Review, Training.

Development Plan. This document outlines the areas of an employee's performance that need improvement. It includes expected results, actions and plans to accomplish the results and a timeframe for performance improvement. Creating a development plan is typically part of the performance review process. Related terms: Development, Education, Learning, Performance Review, Training, Training Strategy.

Dialed Number (DN). The number that the caller dialed to initiate the call.

Dialed Number Identification Service (DNIS). A string of digits that the telephone network passes to the ACD, VRU or other device, to indicate which telephone number the caller dialed. The ACD can then process and report on that type of call according to user-defined criteria. One trunk group can have many DNIS numbers. See Automatic Number Identification.

Dialer. Dialers are technologies (hardware/software) for automating the process of making outbound calls to lists of people. In addition to placing outbound calls, dialers may provide campaign management and scripting functionality, track the disposition of calls and provide detailed real-time and historical reporting.

One way to understand the advantages of using a dialer is to consider it as an ACD for outbound calls. Dialers launch calls and deliver them to agents, just as an ACD does. Dialers also provide tracking, real-time monitoring and reporting capabilities for outbound calls similar to those that ACDs provide for incoming calls.

Dialing modes include:

- Preview dialing: An application that instructs the switch to dial a specific phone number under control of an agent. The agent previews a screen containing information about the person to be called, monitors the call for connection (or other classification), and updates the database accordingly. This is used for callbacks or other contacts in which the agent needs to review information before placing the call. (Vanguard)

- Predictive dialing: An application that instructs the switch to dial multiple simultaneous calls from a preloaded list of phone numbers. A mathematical algorithm is used to predict the correct number of calls to launch based on the expected percentage of completed calls and when agents will become available. It seeks to match the number of completed calls with the number of available agents so that completed calls are immediately handled by an agent. The system determines when a called party has answered and transfers only live calls (and answering machines, if desired) to agents. Agents also receive a data screen about the call. The system classifies all calls launched (e.g., connect, busy, no answer, answering machine, network tones) and updates the database accordingly.

  While some experts claim that predictive dialers can double the total talk time per hour of agents, they offer a trade-off. The more aggressively they are programmed to place calls (and increase "productivity"), the more likely that people will hear silence when they answer the phone, causing more people to hang up. Programming should be done with the objective of increasing completed calls with minimal abandoned calls.

- Progressive dialing: The term is either used as a variation on pre-view dialing or predictive dialing. Some use progressive dialing to describe preview dialing where the preview is timed before automatically launching. Some use progressive dialing to describe a form of controlled predictive dialing where multiple calls are launched only when an agent becomes available. It is still predictive in that it is predicting how many calls will connect. However, it reduces the chance of a live answer by a customer when no agent is available.

- Call blending: The ability to dynamically allocate call center agents to both inbound and outbound calling, based on conditions in the call center and programmed parameters. This enables a single agent to handle both inbound and outbound calls, from the same position, without manually monitoring call activity and reassigning the position. The outbound dialing application monitors inbound calling activity and assigns outbound agents to outbound calling when the inbound volume drops off.

Dialers are evolving from stand-alone systems to become part of integrated call center systems, especially as part of CTI applications. Related terms: Abandoned Rate (Outbound), Completed Call.

Dialog Manager. See Scripting.

Digital. The use of a binary code – 1s and Os – to represent information.

Digital Audio Tape (DAT). Refers to a digital tape recorder and player. There are different types of DAT recorders, players and associated tape cassettes.

Digital Subscriber Line (DSL). An integrated, digital, high-speed (>384 kbps) Internet access and voice service for small offices and residential users. For call centers, it is an enabling technology for work-at-home (telecommuting) agents. (Vanguard)

Direct Call Processing. See Talk Time.

Direct Distance Dialing (DDD). Permits users to place long-distance calls without the assistance of an operator. Related term: North American Numbering Plan.

Direct Inward Dialing (DID). A network service offering – generally associated with local service – in which a unique set of identifying digits is passed to the customer premises equipment. By mapping each set of digits to an internal extension, the switch can provide direct dialing to a particular extension. See Dialed Number Identification Services. (Vanguard)

Directed Dialog. Speech recognition approach that recognizes what is being said based on guided or structured interactions. The caller is given examples of phrases to use. Also referred to as structured language. See Speech Recognition. Related term: Natural Language. (Vanguard)

Disaster Recovery Plan. The purpose of a disaster recovery plan is to enable managers to avoid or recover expediently from an interruption in the center's operation. Comprehensive plans should include an approved set of arrangements and procedures for facilities, networks, people and service levels.

Typical disaster recovery solutions include:

* Remote sites: Facilities that can provide duplicate services.

* Service bureaus: Companies that are prepared to handle the organization's calls in the event of a crisis.

* Reciprocal agreements: Arrangements between companies to provide backup services for each other.

* Multiple data centers: Centers that provide data redundancy.

* Redundant network facilities: Contracting with multiple carriers to provide long distance services. This may also involve established multiple service entry points into the facility and may include alternative channels (e.g., satellite and fiber), sometimes termed dual network routing plan.

* Multiple prerecorded announcements: Having announcements prerecorded (e.g., "we are currently experiencing technical difficulties") that can be deployed immediately.

Discount Rate. The required rate of return that a firm must achieve to justify its investments. Related terms: Internal Rate of Return, Net Present Value. (*Barron's*)

Disparate Treatment. When an employer treats a person differently because of his or her protected class status. Legally defined in Title VII of the Civil Rights Act of 1964.

Display Board. See Readerboard.

Distributed Call Center. See Virtual Call Center.

Distributed Component Object Model (DCOM). A protocol developed by Microsoft that enables software components to communicate directly over a network. Originally called "Network OLE," DCOM is based on the Open Software Foundation's DCE-RPC specification and is designed for use across various network transports, including HTTP.

Divestiture. See Modified Final Judgment.

Double Jack. The ability to plug two headsets into one telephone or workstation so that two people can listen to or participate in the same contact. Often used for side-by-side monitoring. Related terms: Monitoring, Headset.

Downtime. The time that a system is unavailable. This is the most fundamental measure of accessibility. For example, inbound telephone systems are expected to be operational 99.999 percent of the time, which is commonly referred to as "five nines." Computer systems have not historically achieved this level of reliability, but are getting much better. (Vangaurd)

Driver-Based Forecasting. A form of explanatory forecasting. Any method of workload forecasting that is based on other identified activities or "drivers." For instance, a wireless service provider might base volume forecasts for a given month on the number of projected active accounts for the month, the number of new sales anticipated for the month, and the estimated number of cancellations to be received during the month. See Forecasting Methodologies.

Dual-Tone Multifrequency (DTMF). A signaling system that sends pairs of audio frequencies to represent digits on a telephone keypad. It is often used interchangeably with the term Touchtone (an AT&T trademark).

Dumb Switch. A switch that contains only basic hardware and software, and receives call-handling instructions from another device.

Dumb Terminal. A phrase used to describe the user device (terminal) in a computing environment where all of the processing occurs on a central computer or mainframe. No computing intelligence resides on the terminal. See Desktop Technologies. (Vanguard)

Dynamic Answer. An ACD feature that automatically reconfigures the number of rings before the system answers calls based on real-time queue information. Since costs don't begin until the ACD answers calls, this feature can save callers or the call center money on long-distance charges.

Dynamic Data Exchange (DDE). A Microsoft function allowing information from one application to be transferred to another via the Windows operating system. Also referred to as "copying and pasting" or "cut and paste," it involves the temporary storage of information in the Windows Clipboard. (Vanguard)

E1 Circuit. See T1 Circuit.

Economic Development Agency (EDA). Local EDAs can help organizations acquire information on regional demographics, put management in touch with local resources (e.g., colleges and local exchange carriers,), and help secure tax breaks and streamlined regulatory approval for new construction. Related term: Site Selection.

Education. Learning related to future roles or positions for which the individual is being prepared. Education should relate to career-pathing and succession planning. Education has a short- and long-term focus. Related terms: Development, Learning, Training.

Electronic Board. See Readerboard.

Electronic Customer Relationship Management (eCRM). See Customer Relationship Management.

Electronic Documentation. Documentation for an application, product or process that would normally be in the form of paper documentation, but is converted into digital format for display on a desktop computer. (Vanguard)

Electronic Mail (Email). The transmission of information in electronic form from one person (or system) to another over the Internet or other computer network. May refer to the system used to send these messages or the message itself. Can be used to send correspondence such as memos, letters, graphics or electronic files from one computer to another.

Email Response Management System (ERMS). An ERMS controls the flow and tracking of email into an organization in much the same way that an ACD controls the flow and tracking of inbound calls. An ERMS can perform the following routing and reporting functions:

- Conditional routing based on skills, customer priority, etc.
- Priority queuing
- Response time tracking
- Management reporting

However, an ERMS can go much further than an ACD in that it can "read" the subject and/or text of the message and then perform further steps based on business rules. The types of functionality provided by this artificial intelligence include:

- Advanced auto acknowledgment: An automatic response is sent to the sender indicating that the email has been received, along with the timeframe in which to expect a response.

- Recommended response: Incoming email messages are interpreted by the system to determine content and an agent is provided with a recommended response.

- Automated response: Inbound email messages are interpreted by the system to determine content and an automatic response is sent to the customer. (Note: Accuracy rates are often well below 50 percent.)

Further, ERMS vendors are continually upgrading their products. Some of the more advanced features include:

- Multiple language support
- Text-chat capabilities (using the same knowledge base for responses)
- ERMS capabilities delivered via an application service provider

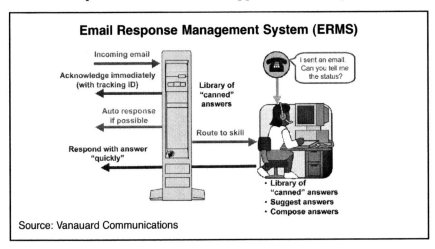

Email Response Management System (ERMS)

Source: Vanauard Communications

The ERMS offers a call center three main benefits:

- Control over email (routing and content)
- Reduction in the staff required to handle it
- Tracking of response times

The relative value of these benefits is typically dependent on the volume of email received in the center and the emphasis placed on quality and service to the customer. Related terms: Automatic Call Distributor, Response Time, Response Time Calculations. (Vanguard)

Employee Satisfaction. As a measure, assigns a value to how satisfied call center employees are with their jobs. Studies have demonstrated that customer satisfaction increases as agent job satisfaction increases. Further, retention, productivity and quality often have a definable, positive correlation to agent satisfaction. Results of surveys to gauge agent satisfaction should be compared to job satisfaction levels in other parts of the organization. Results are typically provided in summarized hard copy, and are often compiled by parties outside of the call center.

Optimizing employee satisfaction is an important success factor in any call center. How employees feel about their jobs can have a significant impact on absenteeism, turnover, customer satisfaction, productivity and overall call center performance.

Employee satisfaction surveys are typically conducted once or twice a year and are good ways to gather feedback quickly and, if desired, anonymously. It is advisable to ask quantitative questions that are easily summarized as well as qualitative questions that may help explain some of the quantitative results. Conducting focus groups can also be an effective way to get feedback on employee satisfaction. However, it may be best to bring in an unbiased, outside firm to conduct the feedback sessions since employees may be less than candid in front of call center management.

Before surveys or focus groups take place, employees should be aware of how the results will be communicated and whether or not actions to improve problems will be taken. Collecting this type of feedback from employees typically produces an expectation that management will take action to improve job satisfaction. See Employee Satisfaction Survey.

Employee Satisfaction Survey. An instrument designed to determine which aspects of employees' work situations contribute to or impede their job satisfaction. Typical areas of measurement include management effectiveness, peers/team members effectiveness, career opportunities, equity of salary, level of appreciation, satisfaction with benefits, and quality of training, feedback and coaching. To conduct a successful employee satisfaction survey, the call center manager should:

- Tell employees the purpose of the survey
- Tell employees how the results will be used
- Inform employees of the results and actions to be taken
- Use data for stated purpose only
- Use the results as a baseline for trending employee satisfaction
- Use a third party to conduct and analyze the survey

See Employee Satisfaction.

Empowerment. To empower someone is to give him or her the official authority to accomplish something. Once individuals are given the opportunity and resources to take control of customer relationships, enhance processes and procedures, and continually improve, they are more likely to become committed to the mission of call center and the organization. Giving people more power and authority does not negate the authority of the manager. Empowerment encourages individuals to expand their knowledge and involvement, and to work with the manager in a quest to enhance performance and customer loyalty. The manager becomes more of a coach, mentor, enabler – focusing on giving individuals what they need, then stepping out of the way to let them do their job. The manager is still, ultimately, accountable for call center performance, but responsibility and authority are shared.

Enterprise Interaction Management (EIM). See Customer Relationship Management.

Enterprise Relationship Management (ERM). See Customer Relationship Management.

Enterprise Resource Planning (ERP). A large-scale business application or set of applications that encompass some or all aspects of back-office functions. There is an evolution within the ERP industry to either provide add-on modules or integrate with third-party applications for front-office functions such as sales, marketing and service. Applications that combine these front-office functions are generally referred to as customer relationship management applications. Related terms: Back Office, Customer Relationship Management, Front Office. (Vanguard)

Envelope Strategy. A scheduling approach whereby enough agents are scheduled for the day or week to handle both the inbound call load and other types of work. Priorities are based on the inbound call load. When call load is heavy, all agents handle calls, but when it is light, some agents are reassigned to work that is not as time-sensitive.

Environmental Scan. An environmental scan surveys the landscape in which an organization conducts business in order to determine the current status of a specific issue or predict future trends. The objective of environmental scanning is to provide management with information that will assist them in planning for the future. For call centers, environmental scans can help anticipate customer expectations and requirements, and secure a common awareness of changing trends among decision makers. The process for conducting an environmental scan includes:

- Identify the issue to be examined
- Identify the industry or discipline that will be reviewed

- Identify the selected materials that will be analyzed
- Ask the right questions
- Examine the facts
- Make recommendations based on the results

Related terms: Business Environment, Customer Survey.

Equal Pay Act (U.S.). The Equal Pay Act of 1963 mandates that men and women are to receive the same pay for doing the same job. Jobs that are the same in terms of skill, effort, working conditions and responsibilities should be compensated equally regardless of the employee's gender. However, individuals can receive different pay for the same position based on one of the following:

- Merit: You can compensate an individual more if he or she is performing better.
- Productivity: Pay differences are allowed for differences in quality and quantity of work.
- Seniority: Compensation plans based on an employee's tenure are permitted.
- Other: Factors such as extra job responsibilities, work shifts and different geographical areas can be compensated differently, as long as gender is not considered.

Equity. The value of the funds contributed by the stockholders plus the retained earnings (or losses).

Equivalent Days. A method of accounting for the differences in the number of days in a month as well as the breakdown of those days (# of Mondays, Tuesdays, etc.) so that comparative analysis of monthly data is more accurate.

Ergonomics. The science of fitting the job to the worker. Ergonomics can prevent work-related cumulative trauma disorders (CTDs) that result when there is a mismatch between the physical capacity of workers and the physical demands of their jobs.

Erlang. One hour of telephone traffic in an hour of time. For example, if circuits carry 120 minutes of traffic in an hour, that's two Erlangs. Related terms: Erlang B, Erlang C, A.K. Erlang (listed as Erlang, A.K.), Queue Dynamics.

Erlang, A.K. A Danish engineer who worked for the Copenhagen Telephone Company in the early 1900s and developed Erlang B, Erlang C and other telephone traffic engineering formulas. Related terms: Erlang, Erlang B, Erlang C.

Erlang B. A formula widely used to determine the number of trunks required to handle a known trunk load during a one-hour period.

Erlang B

Where
A = total traffic in erlangs
N = number of trunks
P = grade of service

$$P = \frac{\dfrac{A^N}{N!}}{\displaystyle\sum_{x=0}^{N} \dfrac{A^x}{x!}}$$

The formula assumes that if callers get busy signals, they go away forever, never to retry ("lost calls cleared"). Since some callers retry, Erlang B can underestimate trunks required. However, Erlang B is generally accurate in situations with few busy signals. Related terms: Erlang, Erlang C, Queue Dynamics, Trunk Load.

Erlang C. A mathematical tool used to calculate predicted waiting times (delay) based on three things: the number of servers (agents); the number of people waiting to be served (callers); and the average amount of time it takes to serve each person. It can also predict the resources required to keep waiting times within targeted limits. Erlang C assumes no lost calls or busy signals, so it has a tendency to overestimate staff required.

Erlang C

Where
A = total traffic offered in erlangs
N = number of servers in a full availability group
P(>0) = probability of delay greater than 0
P = probability of loss – Poisson formula

$$P\,(>0) = \frac{\dfrac{A^N}{N!} \cdot \dfrac{N}{N-A}}{\displaystyle\sum_{x=0}^{N-1} \dfrac{A^x}{x!} + \dfrac{A^N}{N!} \cdot \dfrac{N}{N-A}}$$

Erlang C is widely used in workforce management software programs, as well as low-cost call center staffing calculators. Related terms: Computer Simulation, Erlang, Erlang B, Queue Dynamics.

Error Rate. The number or percentage of defective (e.g., incomplete) transactions or the number or percentage of defective steps in a transaction.

Errors and Rework. As a measurement, the percent (and types) of errors and rework that are occurring. Specific components of errors and rework are often built into quality objectives for agents. However, because not all errors are within their control, variables must be selected carefully. Data generally comes from a database system (customer information system) and/or by ACD call coding. It's appropriate in all environments as a high-level objective; reported monthly or (with the right systems) as often as the manager chooses.

Errors lead to rework, unreliable data and potential interpretation problems downstream. As with first-call resolution, there is significant value in analyzing increases and decreases in errors and rework, in response to changes in processes, systems and other factors. Related terms: Call Quality, First-Call Resolution, System of Causes.

Escalation Plan. A plan that specifies actions to be taken when the queue begins to build beyond acceptable levels. See Real-Time Management.

Ethernet. A standard networking technology for putting information on a local area network. The IEEE standards body defines it, and it is the most popular LAN technology today. It is implemented with network interface cards and ethernet switches and hubs, and it is tightly tied to TCP/IP. (Vanguard)

Event-Driven Forecasting. Any method of workload forecasting that is based on single activities that generate call volume. For example, an insurance company that raises rates for a group of clients might consider the mailing notification of the rate increase to be a special event and will project this volume separately from the normal "ongoing" call volume. See Forecasting Methodologies.

Exchange Line. See Trunk.

Executive Summary. A brief abstract of the key points of a more detailed report or study.

Exempt Employee. A salaried employee not covered by the overtime requirements in the U.S. Fair Labor Standards Act. Includes most administrative, professional, executive and sales jobs; however, the Act should be consulted for specific guidelines on determining exempt employees. Related terms: Fair Labor Standards Act, Nonexempt Employee.

Expected Wait Time (EWT). A formula that uses real-time and/or historical queue data to approximate how long a caller will have to wait for an agent. The system can then take actions based on the predictions (e.g., to play certain messages, route to an IVR, queue for a specific agent group). (Vanguard)

Expert System. Also known as a knowledge-based system. A business application that aids the user in analyzing and resolving problems based on logic trees and known solutions to identified problems. Includes functions such as problem analysis and problem resolution. (Vanguard)

Explanatory Forecasting. See Forecasting Methodologies.

Extensible Markup Language (XML). A language derived from the Standard Generalized Markup Language (SGML) primarily used to pass information between Web pages, applications or systems. A standard for passing data that provides the definition of the type and format of the data, as well as the data, in information passed between systems and applications. Enables very open interchanges between systems. (Vanguard)

External Hiring. Hiring for open positions from outside the call center or organization. The costs and resource implications of whether to hire internally (internal hiring) or externally are specific to each situation. For example, it may be more cost-effective to hire an outside candidate who already possesses required skills than to train an internal employee. However, if recruiting costs are expected to be high and the process of finding the right person long, training an internal hire could be the better solution. Related term: Internal Hiring.

External Turnover. See Turnover.

Extranet. Networks typically connected via the Internet, providing for direct and secure business-to-business access between suppliers and vendors or other partners. (Vanguard)

Extraprise. Refers to a business entity that includes a company, its business partners and suppliers, and its customers. (Vanguard)

Facsimile (FAX). Technology that scans a document, encodes it, transmits it over a telecommunications circuit, and reproduces it in original form at the receiving end. Related terms: Fax on Demand, Fax Server.

Fair Labor Standards Act (U.S.). The Fair Labor Standards Act (FLSA) of 1938, which has been amended numerous times, is designed to protect workers from unfair wage and compensation practices and outlines detailed guidelines for ensuring employees are compensated fairly for the time they work. Far-reaching in scope, the FLSA covers:

- Standards for employee vs. contractor status
- Standards for exempt and nonexempt employee status
- Federal minimum wage and overtime requirements
- Restrictions on the employment of children
- Requirements for human resources record keeping

Family and Medical Leave Act (U.S.). The Family and Medical Leave Act (FMLA) of 1993 requires employers to provide up to 12 weeks of unpaid leave for childbirth or adoption; care of a sick spouse, child or parent; or serious health problems that interfere with job performance.

Fast Clear Down. A caller who hangs up immediately after hearing a delay announcement. Related term: Delay Announcement.

Fault Tolerant. The ability for a system or piece of equipment to keep working even if it encounters a hardware failure. Related term: Disaster Recovery Plan.

Fax. See Facsimile.

Fax on Demand. A system that enables callers to request documents, using their telephone keypads. The selected documents are delivered to the fax numbers they specify. Related terms: Facsimile, Fax Server.

Fax Server. Fax-processing systems have the ability to capture, store, manipulate and recreate analog signals. They can be combined on a single platform, but typically are offered by different suppliers to meet a diversity of business applications. Call centers have, in most cases, moved from fax machines to fax servers and software solutions running on standard hardware platforms. These LAN-based systems provide inbound and outbound capabilities. Some systems automatically distribute incoming faxes or transfer them to an image processing system for retrieval by an agent.

New transmission strategies, often using the Internet or Internet protocols (IP) over private networks, dramatically cut transmission costs by converting fax signals into "packetized" data. A new standard is emerging for IP fax that is more effective than existing standards, and will also support current equipment through gateways. Further, new gateways are emerging that enable many advanced features – even for users with ordinary fax machines. Such features include the ability to:

- Capture and deliver email messages to fax machines
- Route fax traffic on and off the Internet
- Provide advanced reporting, security, guaranteed delivery and receipt
- Provide broadcast functions

Related terms: Facsimile, Fax on Demand.

Federal Communications Commission (FCC). A board of commissioners appointed by the president of the United States. Formed under the Communication Act of 1934, the FCC has the power to regulate interstate and foreign electrical communication systems originating in the United States.

Fiber Optics. Thin filaments of transparent glass or plastic that use light to transmit voice, video or data signals.

First-Call Resolution. The percentage of calls that do not require any further contacts to address the customer's reason for calling. The customer does not need to contact the call center again to seek resolution, nor does anyone within the organization need to follow up.

There is wide variation in the call center industry on how first-call resolution is actually calculated. The basic concept is simple (calls resolved upon initial contact divided by total calls), but the definition of "resolved" or "total calls" can change the results significantly. Because the definition of "resolved on the first call" will vary from call center to call center, benchmarking data on first-call resolution present interpretation challenges for call center managers. Some of the definitions of "resolved" include:

- Caller states, upon being asked, that his/her reason for calling was resolved
- Agent has no follow-up work to do as a result of the call
- Agent does not need to transfer the call
- Agent resolves all of the caller's concerns that fall within the call center's defined responsibility
- One of the call tracking codes designated to count as "resolved" is associated with the call

There are also differences in methods of measuring total calls, including:

- Calls answered
- Calls answered plus calls abandoned
- Calls offered
- Calls answered that meet certain criteria (e.g., omit wrong numbers, calls with invalid data from a call tracking system, calls handled entirely by IVR or calls that the call center is not authorized to resolve)

Ideally, first-call resolution should be defined from the customer's perspective as an issue resolved on first contact (the caller doesn't have to contact the center again or vice versa), even if escalated or transferred during the contact. Transferred/escalated calls can be tracked as supporting data.

First-call resolution and the related measure of "errors and rework" are lasting outgrowths of the quality movement. Studies indicate that companies incur all sorts of additional expenses (many hidden and difficult to track) when callers' issues are not fully resolved with the first call. First-call resolution can be used as a management indicator to drive down costs and improve operational efficiency. This KPI's greatest value is likely to be as a relative measure over time. Related term: Errors and Rework.

Fishbowl. A team decision-making technique in which seating is arranged in two circles – the inner circle (invited group) of persons who discuss the topic/issue and the outer circle (host group) of those who observe. This allows those in the invited group to discuss the topic in an uninterrupted way while the host group observes, listens and learns. When the invited group concludes its discussion, the host group explains what they heard.

Flat Organizational Design. See Organizational Design.

Flat-Rate Service. Services that are priced for a fixed rate, regardless of the amount of usage.

Flex-Time Scheduling. Several weeks in advance, agents are promised schedules within a window of time (e.g., only Tuesdays through Saturdays or from 8 a.m. to 8 p.m. any day of the week), according to their personal availability. Then, specific work hours, and in some cases, days worked, are determined from week to week as forecasted staff requirements are refined. This approach may involve the entire staff, but usually includes only a subset of employees.

Floor Plan Design. The design and layout of call center space (i.e., how workstations are arranged, location of the equipment room, break rooms, training areas and support offices). The floor design affects the placement of power, voice/data lines and heating, ventilation and air conditioning (HVAC), as well as the facility's appearance, costs and ease of change. According to Brendan Read in *Designing the Best Call Center for Your Business* (CMP Books, 2000), a typical sizing approach for calculating the number of agent workstations is to use 90 to 140 square feet per agent.

Flow Chart. A flow chart is a "map" of a process that is used to analyze and standardize procedures, identify root causes of problems and plan new processes. Flow charts are also excellent communication tools, and can help you to visualize and understand the flow of a process.

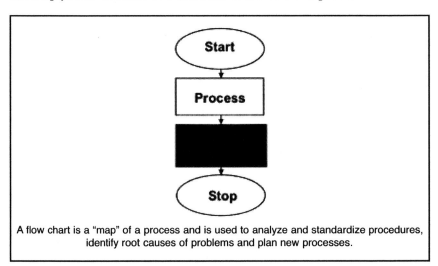

A flow chart is a "map" of a process and is used to analyze and standardize procedures, identify root causes of problems and plan new processes.

One of the most useful applications for a flow chart is to analyze the specific types of transactions you handle. Even a simple transaction consists of many steps. To really understand a transaction, especially the more complex variety, it is necessary to chart what happens step by step. Example applications:

- Transactions, step by step
- The planning and management process
- IVR and ACD programming
- Key procedures
- Related term: System of Causes.

Flushing out the Queue. A real-time management term that refers to changing system thresholds so that calls waiting for an agent group are redirected to another group with a shorter queue or available agents. Related term: Real-Time Management.

Force Field Analysis. This decision-making process involves identifying the factors that support (driving forces) or work against (restraining forces) a proposed plan. This tool is appropriate for determining if the positives outweigh the negatives. Strategies are then developed to strengthen the driving forces and to diminish or eliminate the restraining forces.

Forecasted Call Load vs. Actual. This is a performance objective that reflects the percent variance between the call load forecasted and the call load actually received. It is appropriate in all environments as a high-level objective, reported by interval. It is also used for ongoing tactical adjustments. Forecasted call load is available from the system used for forecasting (e.g., workforce management system or spreadsheets). Actual call load is tracked by the ACD, workforce management system, email response management system, Web servers, etc. – wherever actual data is available.

Forecasting the call load is a high-leverage activity that is fundamental to managing a call center effectively. Underestimating demand will mask and defeat all other efforts to provide good service. And overestimating demand results in waste. Forecasting accuracy should not be reported as a summary of forecasted versus actual calls across a day, week or month, but as an illustration of accuracy for each reporting interval (typically half-hours). Related term: Forecasting Methodologies.

Forecasting. The process of predicting call center workload and other activities. See Forecasted Call Load vs. Actual and Forecasting Methodologies.

Forecasting Methodologies. General methods used to predict future events, such as the amount of workload that will come into an incoming call center in future time periods. Methodologies are broadly categorized into quantitative and judgmental approaches.

Quantitative forecasts include:

- Time-series forecasts, which assume past data will reflect trends that continue into the future. Time-series approaches are common in workforce management software. Time-series forecasting methods include simple or "naive" rules (e.g., the forecast equals last year's same month, plus 12 percent), decomposition, simple time series and advanced time series methods. The governing assumption behind time-series forecasting is that past data will reflect trends that will continue into the future (see chart). Time-series methodologies are common in workforce management software. Most time-series forecasts are reasonably accurate when projecting out three months or less.

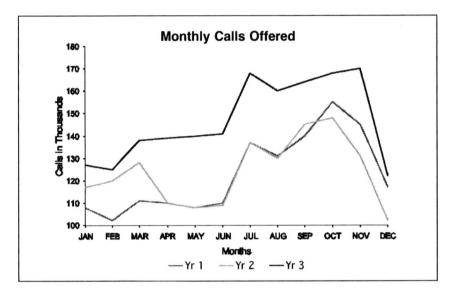

- Explanatory forecasting methods include simple regression analysis, multiple regression analysis, econometric models and multivariate methods. Explanatory forecasting essentially attempts to reveal a linkage between two or more variables. For example, if you manage an ice cream shop, you could statistically correlate the weather (e.g., outside temperature) to ice cream sales; in a call center, you might correlate a price increase to the impact on calling volumes.

Driver-based and event-driven forecasting approaches are variations of explanatory forecasting. Driver-based forecasting assesses other activities that occur across the organization; for example, a wireless service provider might base workload forecasts on the number of projected active accounts for the month, the number of new sales anticipated for the month, and the estimated number of cancellations to be received during the month. Event-driven forecasting is based on single activities that generate call volume; e.g., when a software company releases a new version of software to the market.

Judgmental forecasts go beyond purely statistical techniques. They involve intuition, interdepartmental committees, market research and executive opinion. Some judgment is inherent in virtually all forms of forecasting, and good judgment can significantly improve accuracy. The key is to combine quantitative and judgmental approaches effectively, and to be aware of the limitations of each. Related terms: Driver-Based Forecasting, Forecast, Forecasted Call Load vs. Actual.

Foreign Exchange Line (FX). Provides local telephone service from a central office (CO) to a location outside the CO's serving area. In call center applications, FX lines can give dispersed callers local numbers to dial, while contacts come into a central call center.

Frame Relay. A wide area network data transmission service for connecting multiple local area networks. Enabled by routers, this service is obtained from local and long-distance phone companies, as well as Internet Service Providers. (Vanguard)

Frequency Response. See Headset.

Front Office. Business applications that deal with customer interactions, such as customer service, help desk, sales or customer relationship management. Related terms: Back Office, Enterprise Resource Planning. (Vanguard)

Fulfillment. The processes, systems and people associated with fulfilling orders, requests for information, etc. Fulfillment can be a manual or automated process, or some combination, and the information and/or products can be sent electronically (e.g., via email or fax) or by a shipper. (Vanguard)

Full-Time Equivalent (FTE). A term used in scheduling and budgeting whereby the number of scheduled hours is divided by the hours in a full work week. The hours of several part-time agents may add up to one FTE. FTE should not be confused with:
- Headcount (the number of staff employed)
- Agent seats (the number of workstations available for agents)
- Full-time staff (full-time staff work 40 hours per week)

A full work week (e.g., 40 hours per week) represented by one weekly FTE may be contributed by one person working 40 hours, two people working 20 hours, four people working 10 hours, 40 people working one hour, etc. Related terms: Base Staff, Queue Dynamics, Rostered Staff Factor.

Gantt Chart. See Project Management.

Gap Analysis. The difference between vision (where you want to go) and reality (how things really are). Gap analysis may be used for human resource issues (e.g., the difference between the skills and knowledge available with current staff versus those that are required to accomplish the organization's vision); processes (e.g., the gap between current processes and those required to fulfill the organization's vision); technologies (those that are in place versus those required to enable the organization to achieve its vision); or strategy (current strategy versus required strategy). Related term: System of Causes.

Gate. See Agent Group.

Gateway. A server dedicated to providing access to a network. Also, software and hardware that interprets and translates different protocols from different networks or devices. (Vanguard)

Geographic-Oriented Organizational Design. See Organizational Design.

Grade of Service (GOS). The probability that a call will not be connected to a system because all trunks are busy. Grade of service is often expressed as "p.01" meaning 1 percent of calls will be "blocked." Sometimes, grade of service is used interchangeably with service level, but the two terms have different meanings. Related terms: Erlang B, Service Level, Trunk Load.

Goal. The point of arrival, or the tangible component of a performance objective (e.g., a performance objective may be to reduce turnover by 20 percentage points; if turnover is currently 40 percent, then 20 percent is the goal.) See Performance Objective.

Graphical User Interface (GUI). A computer interface that is graphical in nature, and uses menus, icons and a mouse to enable the user to interact with the system. Web browsers and the Windows and Apple operating systems are examples of GUI interfaces.

Group Interview. Also called team interview. An interview that involves a select group of people conducting the interview together. An interview structure and protocol is established to ensure the required qualifications and characteristics are assessed. Ratings and perspectives are discussed after the interview. Team interviews can save time. They allow the candidate to be interviewed by a variety of people, and enable a diverse evaluation of the applicant's suitability for the position. Related term: Individual Interview.

H.248. An ITU standard, also known as Megaco, for defining the components of a voice switching system. It is also referred to as the "softswitch" standard. It disaggregates a monolithic voice switch into gateways, software controllers and protocols. (Vanguard)

H.323. An ITU standard for putting real-time information onto an unreliable packet network. This standard is the base for most VoIP applications today. Related term: Session Initiation Protocol. (Vanguard)

Handled Call. A call that is received and handled by an agent or peripheral equipment. Related terms: Answered Call, Offered Call, Received Call.

Handling Time. The time an agent spends in talk time and after-call work handling a transaction. Handling time can also refer to the time it takes for a machine to process a transaction. See Average Handling Time.

Hard-Dollar Benefits. See Hard-Dollar Savings.

Hard-Dollar Savings. Sometimes called hard-dollar benefits, refers to savings that can be quantified and that directly impact the bottom line. For example, eliminating overtime or negotiating a better contract for 800 service will result in hard-dollar savings. Soft-dollar savings are difficult to quantify (even though they may be very real); e.g., a more efficient forecasting process that provides planners with more time to improve forecast accuracy.

Hardware. The physical components of a computer system.

Headset. The device that consists of an earpiece and a microphone, and replaces a telephone handset. Headsets are designed to fit comfortably on the user's head, freeing both hands.

Headset performance, design and durability are important contributors to agent productivity. Agents should be able to hear and be heard clearly and feel comfortable in their headsets. A noise-canceling headset has technology that eliminates background noise.

Choosing the right headset involves understanding not only how features can benefit the call center, but also how performance factors impact headset investment over time. Sound quality is one of the most important factors of headset performance.

One of the most important measurements of sound quality is frequency response or bandwidth capability – the percentage of the telephone voice signal delivered after the sound travels over a local or long-distance network. Normally, the network degrades higher frequencies, which gives voice distortion on the receiving end. Therefore, a good headset has a quality microphone that transmits the greatest frequency response, better matching the sound to the original input.

A second factor affecting sound quality is static electricity. As headsets move, they can generate static electricity. Unless the headset has static-resistant components, the static that builds with constant use creates noise on the line. To avoid this, headsets should be designed to resist and eliminate static.

Headset wearers also have a choice of single- and dual-speaker wearing styles, e.g., binaural (earpiece for both ears) or monaural (earpiece for one ear). In noisy call centers, binaural headsets help the agent to focus on the caller. But not every call center needs binaural; in some call centers, being able to hear surrounding sounds from one ear is important.

Heating, Ventilation and Air Conditioning (HVAC). Refers to the systems that control the climate (heating, air conditioning and vitalization) in a building. Some of the components of HVAC systems include air distribution systems, central cooling plants, compressors, condensers, cooling towers, fans and pumps, valves and dampers, zone controls and others. HVAC systems are an important part of facilities design and maintenance.

Help Desk. A term that generally refers to a call center that provides technical support (e.g., to handle queries about product installation, usage or problems). The term is most often used in the context of computer software and hardware support centers. Related terms: Call Center, Internal Help Desk.

Help Desk Software. Applications that deal with customer interactions, usually of a technical nature (e.g., computer support). These applications not only capture and manage contact information but also track and manage problems from initial request to resolution. Often have links to an expert system for the purpose of problem analysis and resolution, and workflow for escalation and follow up. (Vanguard)

Historical Forecasting. Any method of call volume forecasting that relies solely on past call volume to determine future projections. Forecasts from workforce management systems generally rely on historical forecasting. See Forecasting Methodologies.

Historical Report. A report that tracks call center and agent performance over a period of time. Historical reports are generated by ACDs, third-party ACD software packages, and peripherals such as VRUs and call detail recording systems. The amount of history that a system can store varies by system. See Real-Time Report.

Holding Time. See Average Holding Time on Trunks.

Home Agent. See Remote Agent.

Hotline. A call center set up to handle emergency or urgent calls (e.g., an accident hotline).

Human Resources (HR). Refers either to the persons employed in an organization (personnel) or the profession of personnel recruitment and management.

Hunt Group. Basic circular or linear distribution of calls to a group of agents. (Vanguard)

Hybrid. A voice switch application infrastructure approach from PBX vendors that uses an external server attached to the PBX to provide the application software capabilities (routing, work state management, etc.). (Vanguard)

Hyper-Text Markup Language (HTML). A language derived from the Standard Generalized Markup Language (SGML), primarily used to create Web pages. (Vanguard)

Hyper-Text Transport Protocol (HTTP). A protocol in the Web environment that links addresses with a Web server and presents the appropriate HTML pages. (Vanguard)

Identified Ringing. A telephone system feature that provides distinctive ringing sounds for different types of calls.

Idle Time. The inverse of occupancy. The time agents are available and waiting for contacts to arrive. See Occupancy.

Imaging. A technology to scan printed documents such as mail into electronic documents for processing, storage and/or routing. (Vanguard)

Immutable Law. A law of nature that is fundamental and not changeable (e.g., the law of gravity). In an inbound call center, the fact that occupancy goes up when service level goes down is an immutable law. See Queue Dynamics.

In-Band Signaling. Passing information about a contact in the same channel as the voice information. For example, caller ID into a home uses in-band signaling, sending the information between ringing cycles. (Vanguard)

Incentive. Something that motivates efforts, such as the expectation of reward. Good incentive programs are intended to supplement – not replace – a competitive base salary. And each incentive should reward behavior that is linked to the achievement of specific call center/organizational goals.

Incentives come in many different shapes and sizes. Sometimes they represent only a small portion of an agent's total compensation; other times they can contribute to a significant amount of an agent's take-home pay. Examples include merit pay, bonuses, awards and commissions. Incentives can be either team-based or individual. Team incentives reward all members equally based on the performance of the team. Individual incentives are often used when managers feel that higher levels of performance are needed from each member of the team. See Compensation.

Income Statement. Also called the profit-and-loss or P&L statement, summarizes the earnings generated by an organization during a specific period of time. The P&L generally follows a very simple formula: revenue – expenses = net profit. Related terms: Balance Sheet, Cash-Flow Statement, Statement of Retained Earnings.

Incremental Revenue Analysis. A methodology that estimates the value (cost and revenue) of adding or subtracting an agent. This approach determines the potential impact of abandonment because of customer wait time on overall costs; you attach a cost to abandoned calls and make assumptions around how many calls you would lose for various service levels. The theory is that you should continue to add agents and trunks as long as they produce positive incremental (marginal, additional) revenue (value) after paying for their own costs.

Talk Time-180 sec. After Call Work-30 sec. Half Hour's Calls=200 Rostered Staff Factor=1.3		**Incremental Revenue Analysis (Example Only)**									
Agents on Phone	**Rostered Staff (Agentsx1.3)**	**Calls Answered in 20 Sec.**	**% Lost Calls (Assumed)**	**% Calls Lost Forever (Assumed)**	**Trunk Hours**	**Answered Calls**	**Gross Revenue Avg. CAll $22.25**	**Labor Cost $12/hr.**	**Toll-free Trunk Cost 10/Min.**	**Net Revenue**	**$ Increm. Revenue**
25	33	45%	26.0%	7.80%	14.6	184	$4,094	396	88	3610	-
26	34	62%	12.5%	3.75%	12.2	193	$4,294	408	73	3813	203
27	35	74%	6.5%	1.95%	11.2	196	$4,361	420	67	3874	61
28	36	83%	3.5%	1.05%	10.7	198	$4,406	432	64	3910	36
29	38	89%	2.0%	0.60%	10.4	199	$4,428	456	62	3910	0
30	39	93%	1.5%	0.45%	10.3	199	$4,428	468	62	3898	(12)

(Optimum → row 29)

The approach can be a valuable exercise, when used in conjunction with other approaches, as long as the assumptions are understood and communicated to others in the budgeting process. Nevertheless, don't let the scientific look of this approach fool you – it requires some pretty serious guesswork.

Increments. In call centers, increments are the timeframes used for staffing and reporting. Given the variation in workload throughout the day, staff requirements must be calculated at specific increments (which are generally the smallest units of time reflected in the forecast).

Thirty-minute reporting increments are often used as the basis for forecasts and staff calculations because they provide an adequate level of detail and accuracy for most inbound call centers. Call centers that handle long calls (approaching 30 minutes) generally establish report increments and staff calculations around hours. Peaked traffic, which is a surge beyond random variation within a half hour, requires reports and staffing calculations at five- or 10-minute increments. Related terms: Long Call, Peaked Call Arrival, Queue Dynamics, Traffic Arrival.

Incumbent Local Exchange Carrier (ILEC). See Local Exchange Carrier.

Index Factor. In forecasting, a proportion used as a multiplier to adjust another number. For example, in a time-series forecast, Monday's index factor may be 1.2 – meaning that Mondays typically receive 1.2 times (20 percent more than) the average day's call load.

Individual Interview. An interview that follows a traditional format in which the applicant is involved in a conversation with one interviewer at a time. The selection process may consist of a series of individual interviews to factor in several interviewers' impressions of the applicant. Related term: Group Interview.

Information Indicator (II). Also called information indicator digits. Information sent in an ISDN D channel setup message that providers additional information about the call source, such as payphone, cell phone, calling card, prisons and hotels. This information can be used in call centers for advanced routing applications. (Vanguard)

Information Systems (IS). A generic term for systems that perform data processing.

Information Technology (IT). A generic term that refers either to computer and/or communications systems and technologies, or the profession that develops and manages these systems.

Instant Messaging (IM). A form of text-chat used primary for non-commercial communications between two or more Internet users. Several incompatible addressing and protocols issues have limited its use for business-to-business or business-to-consumer applications. (Vanguard)

Institute of Electrical and Electronics Engineers (IEEE). Pronounced "eye-triple-E," the IEEE is a non-profit, technical professional association of electrical and electronics engineers.

Integrated Reporting. The ability to track a call from its inception to culmination and tie business information and results together with call data. Also referred to as cradle-to-grave reporting. Each point the call touches (e.g., IVRs, announcements, agents) and the business results of those transactions (sales, complaints, contact record) are tracked on a single database record and/or via a common tracking identifier. This enables more accurate tracking of caller treatment and contact results. (Vanguard)

Integrated Services Digital Network (ISDN). A set of international standards for telephone transmission. ISDN provides an end-to-end digital network, out-of-band signaling and greater bandwidth than older telephone services. Often used in call centers to deliver signaling information quickly for use of ANI and DNIS, and for faster call setup and tear-down. The two standard levels of ISDN are basic rate interface (BRI) and primary rate interface (PRI). Related terms: Basic Rate Interface, Primary Rate Interface.

I

Intelligent Character Recognition (ICR). Technology that reads handwritten text and determines what it says. Can be used with an imaging system to determine information about mail or fax items for routing and handling. Related term: Optical Character Recognition. (Vanguard)

Intelligent Routing. The use of information about the caller, current conditions or other parameters to route calls to the appropriate group, individual, automated system, etc. DNIS, ANI, customer-entered digits and database information can all be used as routing parameters. It can augment or replace conditional and skills-based routing performed on the switch and is generally enabled via CTI.

Inter-Exchange Carrier (IXC). A long-distance telephone company.

Interactive Voice Response (IVR). A system that enables callers to use their telephone keypad (or spoken commands if speech recognition is used) to access a company's computer system for the purpose of retrieving or updating information, conducting a business transaction, or routing their call. Also referred to as voice response unit (VRU).

IVR systems are in use in a large number of call centers. The term "voice-processing system" is generically used to describe any system that requests any type of caller input; however, there are actually three general terms – each with slightly different meanings – in use today:

- Auto attendant: An auto-attendant system is typically an inexpensive add-on to an ACD and only provides routing capabilities; it does not interact with a database. An auto-attendant is typically used in applications where a caller is asked to "press one for this, two for that."

- Voice response unit (VRU): Often used interchangeably with IVR, the VRU more typically refers to the equipment running the system, rather than the system itself or the capability.

- Interactive voice response (IVR): Systems that enable callers to use a telephone keypad (or spoken commands if speech recognition is used) to access a company's computer system for the purpose of retrieving or updating information, conducting a business transaction or routing calls.

In the past, all of these systems worked by turning the distinct DTMF (dual-tone multifrequency, otherwise known as touchtone) codes created by user input on the phone keypad to data bytes that are understood by the system. This is still the most common methodology in use today. However, speech recognition is fast becoming an easy and desirable way of interacting with these systems.

IVR systems can be placed in front of an ACD via direct trunking or they can be connected behind the switch. Either way, the IVR typically interacts with the caller at the beginning of the call. IVR systems can also be used to conduct caller surveys at the completion of calls.

IVR systems continue to advance, and are increasingly able to handle transactions simply and effectively. Some of the more advanced offerings found today include:

- Fax on demand: The IVR system interacts with the fax server to send forms and other information to a caller without any agent intervention.

- Post-call surveying: Callers are notified up front that a survey is available after the call and are sent to the application upon call completion (to fill out simple surveys that generally last two minutes or less).

- Text-to-speech capability: The IVR "reads and speaks" information contained in a database back to the caller. An example is reading out a name or address to ensure that a correct match has occurred.

- Speech recognition: Rather than relying on DTMF (touchtone) input, the system allows the caller to speak and then turns the spoken words into digital demands that the system can understand.

Related terms: Audiotex, Automated Attendant, Speech Recognition, Voice Processing. (Vanguard)

Interactive Web Response (IWR). Systems that enable customers to use the Internet to access a company's Web site for the purpose of retrieving or updating information or conducting a business transaction. (Vanguard)

Intercept Service. A message service provided by telephone companies to inform users of the status of numbers that are not in service (e.g., no longer in service, number change, invalid number).

Interconnect Company. A company that provides telecommunications systems for connection to the telephone network. The term goes back to the days before divestiture; any vendor other than AT&T that provided systems to customers were interconnect companies.

Interconnect Equipment. Also called terminal equipment or customer-premises equipment. The equipment connected to the telecommunications network.

Interface. Hardware and/or software that allows disparate devices or programs to communicate.

I

Interflow. See Overflow.

Internal Help Desk. A technical support center set up for the employees of a company. Can also mean an agent group that supports other internal agent groups; e.g., for complex or escalated calls. Related terms: Agent Group, Call Center, Help Desk, Internal Response Time.

Internal Hiring. Hiring for open positions from within the organization or call center. See External Hiring.

Internal Part-Timers. A scheduling approach, sometimes called the reinforcement method. When contact-handling duties are combined with other types of tasks, such as correspondence, outbound calling or data-entry, the agents assigned to these collateral duties can act as reinforcements when the calling load gets heavy. This is like being able to bring in part-timers on an hourly, half-hourly or even five-minute basis. Related terms: Schedule, Schedule Alternatives.

Internal Rate of Return (IRR). A capital budgeting method, internal rate of return is similar to the net present value (NPV). Where the NPV uses a fixed discount rate to compare cash flows to the initial investment, the IRR calculates the rate of return of the cash flow. This value can then be compared to the discount rate to determine if the project is viable.

As with the NPV, the IRR can be calculated using tables. However, it is much easier and more effective to calculate the IRR using a spreadsheet program. The following is an example of IRR:

Initial Investment	-115,000
Year	Cash Flow
1	40,000
2	41,000
3	42,000
4	43,000
IRR	16%

If the firm's discount rate is 10 percent, the project can be approved since the IRR (16 percent) is higher than the discount rate. The payback period, NPV and IRR all provide managers with different ways of determining the value of an investment. An understanding of all three methods provides the call center manager with the ability to fully comprehend the financial implications of capital investments. Related Terms: Payback Period, Net Present Value.

Internal Response Time. The time it takes an agent group that supports other internal groups (e.g., for complex or escalated tasks) to respond to transactions that do not have to be handled when they arrive (e.g., correspondence or email). Related terms: Internal Help Desk, Response Time, Response Time Calculation.

Internal Turnover. See Turnover.

International Access Code. The first set of digits required in order to place an international telephone call.

International Organization for Standardization (ISO). A network of national standards institutes from 145 countries working in partnership with international organizations, governments, industry, business and consumer representatives. ISO is the source of the popular ISO 9000 series quality standards. See ISO 9000 Series.

International Telecommunications Union (ITU). Headquartered in Geneva, Switzerland, ITU is an international organization where governments and the private sector coordinate global telecom networks and services. The ITU is a part of the United Nations system of organizations.

Internet. A worldwide, expanding network of linked computers, founded by the U.S. government and several universities in 1969, originally called Arpanet and based on TCP/IP protocol. Made available for commercial use in 1992. (Vanguard)

Internet "Call Me" Transaction. A transaction that allows a user to request a callback from the call center, while exploring a Web page. Requires interconnection of the ACD system and the Internet by means of an Internet gateway.

Internet "Call Through" Transaction. Refers to the ability for callers to click a button on a Web site and be directly connected to an agent (initiate a voice conversation) while viewing the site. Standards and technologies that provide this capability are in development.

Internet Engineering Task Force (IETF). An international community of network designers, operators, vendors and researchers concerned with the evolution of the Internet architecture and the smooth operation of the Internet. The IETF is open to any interested individual.

Internet Phone. Technology that enables users of the Internet's World Wide Web to place voice telephone calls through the Internet, thus bypassing the long-distance network.

Internet Protocol (IP). The set of communication standards that control communications activity on the Internet. An IP address is assigned to every computer on the Internet.

Internet Service Provider (ISP). A company that provides Internet access to customers, either through a modem or direct connection. Related term: Network Service Provider. (Vanguard)

Internet Telephony. See IP Telephony.

Interval Based Accuracy. A method of measuring forecast success that focuses on results by interval (usually half-hours), rather than end of day, week or month results. See Forecasting Methodologies.

Interview. In a hiring context, interviews are conversations between an employer and prospective job candidates. Interviewing provides you with the information to determine those who should continue in the selection process and identify those who are not an appropriate fit. Related terms: Group Interview, Individual Interview, Structured Interview, Unstructured Interview.

Intraday Forecast. A short-term forecast that assumes activities early in the day will reflect how the rest of the day will go. Intraday forecasts are easy to produce and are often quite accurate.

	Intraday Forecasting	
402	Calls received by 10:30 a.m.	
÷ .18	Usual proportion of calls by 10:30 a.m.	
2,233	Revised forecast for day	
x .066	3:30-4:00 p.m. proportion	
147	Intraday forecast for 3:30-4:00 p.m.	

The approach works like this: At some point in the morning, say just after 10:30 a.m., your reports indicate you have received 402 calls so far. Divide the usual proportion of the day's calls that you would expect by 10:30, 18 percent in this case, into 402. (Eighteen percent came from looking at traffic patterns on previous days and calculating half-hourly proportions.) You now know that, if the trend continues, you can expect to receive 2,233 calls for the day, which you can then break down into each remaining increment. See Intraweek Forecast.

Intraflow. See Overflow.

Intranet. A company's private data network that is accessed using browser-based technology and TCP/IP protocol. (Vanguard)

Intraweek Forecast. A short-term forecast that assumes activities early in the week will reflect how the rest of the day will go. Similar to Intraday Forecasting. See Intraday Forecast.

Intraweek Forecasting

3,050	Calls received on Monday
÷ .23	Usual proportion of calls by Monday
13,261	Revised calls forecast for week
x .17	Friday's proportion
2,254	Intraweek forecast for Friday

Invisible Queue. When callers do not know how long the queue is or how fast it is moving. Related terms: Queue, Visible Queue.

Involuntary Turnover. See Turnover.

IP Phone. An end-user device that enables users to place voice calls through a data network (LAN, WAN or the Internet) using the Internet Protocol. The device can be an IP-enabled telephone or a PC with sound-card and software. Either device converts the source information from circuit-switched to packet-switched format. (Vanguard)

IP Telephony. Technology that enables voice telephone calls to be carried over a data network (a private intranet or the public Internet) using protocols from the TCP/IP suite. Voice is transmitted in data packets. Also referred to as Internet telephony. (Vanguard)

ISO 9000 Series. A set of international quality standards developed by the International Organization for Standardization (ISO). Variations in this series include the ISO 9001, 9002 and 9003 compliance standards, which cover various aspects of quality, testing and production. For more information, see www.iso.ch. Related term: International Organization for Standardization.

Java. An object-oriented programming language developed by Sun Microsystems. It is designed for creating and executing operating system independent applications. (Vanguard)

Java Applet. Small Java-based applications that can be downloaded and run within browsers on virtually any operating system without modification, making them ideal for use over the Internet. (Vanguard)

Java Telephony Application Programming Interface (JTAPI). An object-oriented application programming interface for Java-based computer-telephony applications. Allows Java applications to initiate, control and disconnect telephone calls. (Vanguard)

Job Aid. Sources of information pertinent to specific job roles and tasks that can be accessed quickly by employees as needed.

Job Description. A description of the roles, responsibilities and requirements of a specific job. Job descriptions should reflect the mission of the center and be reviewed on a regular basis to ensure they reflect the current expectations of positions. At a minimum, job descriptions should include:

- Job purpose: Summarizes how the position furthers the mission of the organization (i.e., the benefits to the organization's stakeholders, the issues/opportunities addressed by the position and the position's direct and indirect customers).

- Definition of responsibilities: Provides a listing of responsibilities and duties from the most important tasks of the position (i.e., the time generally expected to be allocated between key tasks and how each responsibility supports the department's mission).

- Skills and experience: Identifies and documents the education, skills and experiences required. This enables those involved in recruiting and hiring to speed these processes and ensure that only qualified candidates are considered.

See Job Role.

Job Evaluation. The process of identifying and describing jobs, and determining the relative worth or value of a job to the organization. Traditionally, the six primary steps of the job evaluation process include:

1. Analyze the job
2. Write the job description
3. List the job specifications
4. Rate the job

5. Develop a job hierarchy

6. Classify jobs into grades.

There are many opponents of this traditional job evaluation approach. Concerns with these systems – common in government, large organizations and union environments – generally fall into two categories: 1) they are overly rigid, and 2) pay grades don't accurately reflect fair market value of positions. While any organization needs a consistent approach for determining pay scales and job worth, a trend in many organizations in recent years has been to move away from the most formal, inflexible types of job grading systems. Related terms: Job Description, Job Role.

Job Role. The function or responsibilities related to a specific position in an organization. The table below illustrates how job titles and responsibilities are typically defined in larger call centers. Note, the larger the center, the more specialization around specific responsibilities required. Smaller call centers may combine several areas of responsibility into one job title, or may not have a need for the function at all.

Job	Responsibilities (Large Call Center Example)
Agent	• Identify and handle customer inquiries • Apply customer service policies • Perform business retention activities • Resolve customer problems • Educate customers on products and services offered • Match product benefits with customer needs • Enter coding and tracking information completely and accurately
Team Leader/ Supervisor	• Resolve agent and customer issues • Participate in new-hire interviews • Conduct performance reviews and team meetings • Perform the work of agents during peak periods (in many organizations) • Conduct monitoring and coaching sessions • Coordinate with training and quality assurance to identify systemic quality-improvement opportunities • Represent the team on special projects/initiatives
Technical Support Manager	• Maintain existing software/hardware • Recommend technology solutions • Install technology systems and upgrades • Provide technical assistance to operations

	• Update call-routing tables and systems • Troubleshoot technical problems • Plan and schedule system backup/outages to minimize customer impact
Workforce Manager	• Spearhead the call center planning process • Ensure key planning concepts are understood by the entire organization • Ensure call center and staffing models include accurate, updated information • Conduct meetings with relevant departments regarding forecast and workload requirements • Present key performance results to executive management • Research and recommend vendor and software for forecasting and scheduling activities • Train team leaders, managers and trainers on the use of workforce planning tools (e.g., work modes, schedule adherence, etc.) • Provide executive management with reports on workload trends and staffing requirements
Workforce Analyst	• Develop reports on daily workload • Participate in forecasting meetings with relevant departments; develop accurate short- and long-term workload forecasts • Control master systems files with schedule information and shift preferences • Serve as initial point of contact for all issues regarding schedules • Process day-off requests and update systems • Determine workforce requirements to meet service level and response time objectives • Determine agent schedules to meet call center objectives
Workforce Real-Time Analyst	• Provide intra-day monitoring and reporting • Recommend real-time schedule changes and identify efficiency opportunities • Adjust schedules based on workload/forecast shifts • Update systems with real-time shift adjustment information • Develop and distribute real-time summary reports to management team
Training Manager	• Work with operations to determine new-hire and ongoing training needs • Develop or buy appropriate training courses; implement programs • Determine best methods of delivery

	• Create effectiveness evaluations and update/improve training accordingly • Partner with operations on new initiatives and determine training resources necessary for support
Quality Assurance Manager	• Recommend, implement and direct monitoring program (e.g., side-by-side, silent, remote, mystery shopper, etc.) • Work with managers and supervisors/team leaders to calibrate monitoring processes and results • Research and recommend vendors for automated processes • Gather and distribute results • Align internal monitoring with external customer feedback
Call Center Manager	• Implement call center strategies and tactics • Establish agent and team objectives • Work with the workforce management team to ensure accurate staffing and scheduling • Work with supervisors/team leaders, analysts and support positions to establish and manage priorities • Coordinate with VP/director and other managers to monitor budget requirements and compliance • Conduct supervisor/team leader performance reviews and administer rewards • Provide on-the-job training and mentoring • Oversee recruiting, hiring and training processes
Vice President/ Director	• Collaborate with senior-level management to determine the strategic direction of the call center • Align call center objectives with enterprise and customer objectives • Oversee implementation of strategies • Develop and manage budgets; secure required resources • Determine and communicate the call center's return on investment to the organization • Oversee recruiting, hiring and training of managerial staff • Conduct performance reviews of managers and administer rewards • Champion the call center throughout internal and external channels

Related terms: Job Description, Job Evaluation.

Judgmental Forecasting. Goes beyond purely statistical techniques and encompasses what people believe is going to happen. It is in the realm of intuition, interdepartmental committees, market research and executive opinion. See Forecasting Methodologies.

Key Performance Indicator (KPI). A high-level measure of call center performance. Note, some interpret KPI as the single most important measure in a department or unit; however, in common usage, most call centers have multiple KPIs. See Performance Objective.

Key Telephone System. A small, simple telephone system with a limited number of lines and extensions.

Keypad. The dialing pad of a telephone or other device.

Knowledge Base (KB). A system used to capture, store and process information on customers, products and services.

Knowledge-Based System. See Expert System.

Knowledge Management. According to consultant Jenny McCune, knowledge management is the task of developing and exploiting an organization's tangible and intangible knowledge resources. An organization's tangible assets include such things as copyrights, patents, R&D, licenses and product, customer and competitor information. The intangible assets are the knowledge that the employees possess, including professional know-how, experience, skills, their own processes or methods, personal insight and creative solutions.

The main objective of knowledge management is to leverage and reuse resources that already exist in the organization so people will not spend time "reinventing the wheel." See Learning Organization.

Knowledge Worker. A worker who is involved primarily in "symbolic analysis" – dealing with symbols, concepts and communications, rather than tangible goods. In this sense, many call center agents are knowledge workers.

Law of Diminishing Returns. The law of diminishing returns, common in economics, is a significant consideration in a queuing environment. It can be stated this way: When successive individual agents are assigned to a given call load, marginal improvements in service level that can be attributed to each additional agent will eventually decline.

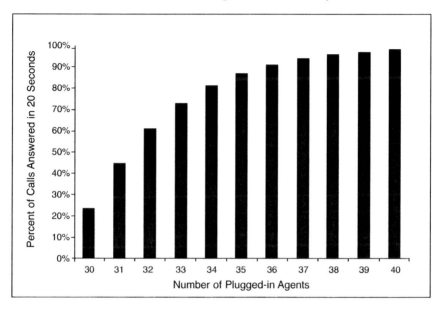

As the graph illustrates, 30 agents at the given call load will provide a service level of just over 24 percent in 20 seconds. With 31 agents, things improve dramatically – service level jumps to 45 percent, a quantum improvement. Adding one more person yields another big improvement. In fact, adding only four or five people takes service level from the depths of poor service to something much more acceptable. Each person has a significant positive impact on the queue when service level is low. Keep adding, though, and the improvements are less dramatic. Related terms: Immutable Law, Queue Dynamics.

Learning. The acquisition of knowledge, skills and abilities. Related terms: Education, Development, Training.

Learning Organization. Harvard Business School Professor David Garvin defines a learning organization as "skilled at creating, acquiring and transferring knowledge, and at modifying its behavior to reflect new knowledge and insights." Learning organizations look at the systems and processes contributing to learning as opposed to focusing primarily on specific interventions, such as a training class. This perspective leads to knowledge management and the successful development of an organization's intellectual capital. Individual learning takes place each time an individual learns; team learning takes place when two or more individuals learn from the same activity; system learning takes place when the organization develops methods to acquire and use organizational knowledge. See Knowledge Management.

Lease. According to *Barron's*, a lease is "a legal contract under which the owner of an asset (lessor) gives another party (lessee) the right to use an asset for a certain period of time in return for specified periodic payments." Many call center vendors offer leases as an alternative to buying equipment. In some cases, leasing can provide an attractive option compared to a purchase.

In deciding whether to purchase or lease, the manager needs to determine the least expensive alternative, generally identified by net present value. The alternative with the lowest (not highest) net present value (NPV) would be the best alternative in this case. The calculation must also take into account tax implications, depreciation schedules and salvage values where appropriate. Related term: Net Present Value.

Least-Occupied Agent. A method of distributing calls to the agent who has the most idle time (lowest occupancy), in a given period of time. Related terms: Longest Available Agent, Next Available Agent. (Vanguard)

Leave Without Pay (LWOP). Agents are offered the chance to leave work early, without pay, when call volumes are low. Pronounced "el-wop." Related terms: Schedule, Schedule Alternatives.

Legacy Systems. Information systems or databases that house vital business information, such as customer records, but are often based on older technologies (e.g., mainframes, mini-computers). (Vanguard)

Liability. A legal debt or obligation of the organization; e.g., loans, accounts payable, mortgages.

Light-Emitting Diode (LED). A device that emits light when connected in a circuit. LEDs are often used as "pilot" lights in electronic systems and appliances to indicate whether or not a circuit is closed.

Line Conditioning. Treating communication channels to reduce distortion and "noise," in order to improve transmission speed and reliability.

Linux. An open source Unix operating system. Some call center applications (e.g., some communications servers) run on Linux. See Unix. (Vanguard)

Liquid Crystal Display (LCD). An alphanumeric display that uses liquid crystal sealed between pieces of glass.

Load Balancing. In a network call center environment, load balancing is the process of distributing (balancing) contacts between call centers. Related terms: Call-by-Call Routing, Network, Network Control Center, Network Interflow, Percent Allocation.

Local Area Network (LAN). The connection of multiple computers within a building so that they can share information, applications and peripherals. Related term: Wide Area Network.

Local Exchange Carrier (LEC). A telephone company responsible for providing local connections and services. New startup LECs are sometimes referred to as competitive local exchange carriers (CLECs), while telephone companies in existence at the time of the breakup of AT&T are known as incumbent local exchange carriers (ILECs).

Local Service Area. A local geographical area that charges the same local rates for telephone services.

Logged On. A state in which agents have signed on to a system (made their presence known), but may or may not be ready to receive calls.

Loggers or Logging Systems. Tools that automatically record and archive calls in a call center. Can be used to record every call, record on demand or conduct event-based recording. Used by companies, such as insurance, financial services and utilities, which must keep detailed records of transactions for verification or legal purposes. Today's systems can record both voice and data screens. (Vanguard)

Logical Agent. An agent identified by their login code, not by their physical position or phone number. This feature enables an agent to login from anywhere in the call center and be recognized by the system the same way for routing and statistics purposes. See Agent Group. (Vanguard)

Long Call. When average handling time approaches or exceeds 30 minutes. Long calls cause problems in call centers that use the typical 30-minute increment for forecasting and staffing. Since long calls are not distributed as Erlang C assumes, they may violate the assumptions of the formula.

Compounding the problem is the fact that ACDs often count calls in the period in which they begin, but report average handling time in the period in which they end. Consequently, reported averages can be skewed. For planning and management purposes, report intervals may need to be adjusted upward to hours. This minimizes the effects of skewed averages since more calls will begin and end in the same reporting period.

If you have long calls, it is also important to balance common sense with statistics. For example, if long calls are an anomaly, you might opt to adjust your statistics before using your reports to project staffing needs. And to avoid a low service level, you may need to force higher staffing in hours when long calls arrive.

Most Erlang C programs will allow you to define the interval you want to examine; e.g., hours instead of half-hours. Alternatively, you can program a simulator to model the mix of calls you are taking.

You will also need to consider how you manage long calls. For example, a second tier of staff may be an efficient way to handle complex calls. Calls to the initial group can be treated normally, all callers reach someone quickly, and those with simple questions don't have to wait for the second tier. Further, those with complex problems may be more willing to wait for service, and agents handling these calls can do so under less pressure. Be sure also to manage the service level of the second group or service in both tiers will suffer. See Increment.

Long-Distance Access Code. A code used to access the network of a specific long-distance carrier.

Longest Available Agent. Also referred to as most-idle agent. A method of distributing calls to the agent who has been sitting idle the longest. With a queue, longest available agent becomes next available agent. Related terms: Least-Occupied Agent, Next-Available Agent.

Longest Delay. Also called oldest call. The longest time a caller has waited in queue, before abandoning or reaching an agent. See Queue Dynamics.

Longitudinal Surveys. Surveys that gather data over a period of time, usually to detect trends. See Customer Survey.

Look-Ahead Queuing. The ability for a system or network to examine a secondary queue and evaluate the conditions before overflowing calls from the primary queue.

Look-Back Queuing. The ability for a system or network to look back to the primary queue after the call has been overflowed to a secondary queue and evaluate the conditions. If the congestion clears, the call can be sent back to the initial queue.

Lost Call. See Abandoned Call.

Mainframe. A computer system that is a large, monolithic system. Generally has its own operating system, and databases and applications resident on the same system. (Vanguard)

Make Busy. To make a circuit or terminal unavailable.

Managed Staffing Arrangement. An arrangement whereby a managed staffing company supplies all or part of the organization's employee needs, according to the organization's business rules and guidelines. Individuals hired are on the managed staffing company's payroll, and administrative responsibilities, feedback and coaching, and disciplinary actions are the responsibility of the staffing company.

This staffing arrangement is a variation of outsourcing, with the managed staffing company using your facilities instead of their own. It is a form of co-sourcing, which generally refers to an outsourcing arrangement whereby the client and the outsourcer partner to provide IT services, call center capabilities, facilities management or other types of services.

Management By Walking Around (MBWA). The practice of managers literally walking around (i.e., being out on the call center floor, in the production plant or in the fulfillment area) so that they can see first-hand what is happening, and can interact with and encourage employees. Popularized by management author Tom Peters in the early 1980s.

Management Information System (MIS). For call centers, a system that facilitates the capture and reporting of activity within the telephony and computing infrastructure. (Vanguard)

Manual Answer. The ACD system is set up so that agents must manually answer calls. See Call Forcing.

Manual Available. The ACD system is set up so that agents must put themselves back into the available mode after completing any after call work. See Auto Available.

Market Environment. See Business Environment.

Market Research. The disciplined process of collecting, analyzing and interpreting information about customers in order to make better decisions about meeting customer needs and expectations. The call center can both benefit from market research and assist in market research efforts. Market research can help call center managers make decisions about servicing customers (e.g., what access channels to offer to different customer segments or how many self-service options should be provided to customers). On the other hand, the call center can contribute to market research since it has a wealth of customer intelligence at its fingertips. The call center should work with other departments in the organization to provide them with the strategic customer data they require to make sound business decisions. See Call Center Value Proposition.

Market Share. The percentage of total sales of a type of product or service that are received by the organization from a particular set of potential buyers. The market share percentage is highly dependant upon how the market is defined.

Matrix Organizational Design. See Organizational Design.

Mean Time Between Failure (MTBF). An estimate of the average time before a system or component will likely fail.

Measurement. A quantifiable unit. In call centers, this generally refers to time (e.g., handle time), an input (e.g., a telephone call, email, customer), an output, (e.g., a sale, proposal, completed contact, problem resolution) or a ratio expressed with a numerator and denominator (e.g., absenteeism, close ratio, first-call resolution).

Media Gateway Control Protocol (MGCP). A protocol designed to bridge the public-switched network with Internet protocol (IP) packet-switched networks.

Mediation. Where opposing sides of a conflict are brought together and work toward a resolution with the help of an intermediary who is called a mediator. Mediation is often used when positive conflict-resolution steps have reached an impasse and communication between the parties has stalled. The mediator is not a judge and does not announce a decision or ruling on the matter at hand. He or she is responsible for assisting the disputing parties toward resuming communication and coming to a mutual agreement.

Megaco. A pending IETF VoIP standard that is the equivalent of the ITU's H.248. The joint IETF/ITU standard is sometimes referred to as Megaco/H.248. (Vanguard)

Mentoring. Professor John Walton describes mentoring as a process whereby experienced and often senior employees support and advise less-experienced and often younger colleagues through their personal and career development. The person being mentored is referred to as the protégé. Mentoring differs from coaching in that it does not focus on a particular set of skills or knowledge; instead, a mentor guides overall career objectives.

Merit Pay. The increase in a person's base pay as a result of good performance.

Merlang. A term used by workforce management vendor Pipkins, which refers to a modified Erlang formula. Related terms: Erlang, Erlang B, Erlang C.

Message Unit. A unit of measurement used in charging for local telephone calls, where applicable.

Metrics. Another word for measurements or, sometimes in usage, objectives. Related terms: Key Performance Indicator, Performance Objective.

Middleware. A generic term for software that mediates between different types of hardware and software on a network so that they can function together. Typically uses open interfaces and applications programming interfaces (APIs) to access and move information. In call centers, middleware is typically used in CRM and CTI application integration. (Vanguard)

Milestone. See Project Management.

Mission. Clarifies the organization's purpose. The mission statement declares why the organization exists, and therefore what it strives to do in every transaction and decision it makes. While the core values describe principles upon which the organization acts and the vision communicates where the organization wants to be, the mission clarifies the organization's purpose.

The mission should be understood by everyone in the organization and should be practiced daily. Core values, vision and mission are three inter-related components of defining and describing an organization's essence. Related terms: Core Values, Mission Statement, Vision.

Mission Statement. A statement that describes the organization's mission in understandable, compelling terms. Effective mission statements convey striking insight in just a few words. They should make sense and inspire commitment. Related terms: Core Values, Mission, Vision.

Modem. A contraction of the terms modulator/demodulator. A modem converts analog signals to digital and vice versa.

Modified Accelerated Cost Recovery System (MACRS). See Depreciation.

Modified Final Judgment. The 1982 agreement reached between the U.S. Justice Department and AT&T that separated AT&T's equipment manufacturing and long-distance businesses from the local exchange companies. It resulted in a divestiture that created separately owned Regional Bell Operating Companies (RBOCs).

Modular Jack. An interface that permits easy interconnection of telecommunications equipment or circuits.

Monitoring. Monitoring is a call evaluation process that appraises the qualitative aspects of call handling. Monitoring programs include the tracking and analysis of data to identify individual agent and overall call center performance trends, anticipated problems, and training and coaching needs. Effective monitoring programs are closely aligned with both individual coaching and overall quality improvement initiatives.

There are several ways to monitor your agents' performance, including:

- Silent Monitoring: The supervisor or person who is responsible for conducting the monitoring session listens to an agent call in real-time from another location. In some call centers, the supervisor can also monitor the agent's keyboard activities, called screen monitoring, to ensure quality and system navigation while the agent is handling the call.

- Call Recording: The supervisor or automated system records a sampling of calls. The person conducting the monitoring then randomly selects calls for evaluation of agent performance.

- Side-by-Side Monitoring: The person conducting the monitoring sits beside the agent and listens while the agent handles a call.

- Peer Monitoring: Call center agents monitor peers' calls and provide feedback on their performance.

- Mystery Shopper: A form of unobtrusive observation in which a designated "mystery shopper" initiates a call to the center and monitors the skills of the agent.

The major objectives and uses of a monitoring program include:

- Provides the basis for organizationwide quality improvement and innovation

- Measures the quality of interaction and accuracy of information provided

- Measures adherence to the call-handling processes

- Contributes to consistency and effectiveness of call center processes

- Provides data for trend analysis to look for patterns of effectiveness across call contact types, teams and centers

- Supports coaching by providing specific examples for feedback
- Identifies additional training needs for individual agents
- Evaluates the effectiveness of training
- Identifies customer needs/expectations
- Supports a tactical deployment of call center and enterprise vision
- Evaluates customer satisfaction
- Refines the selection process in that monitoring helps in the development of a profile of skills and competencies
- Provides legal compliance and mitigates liability
- Ensures agents follow organization's policies

Monitoring is also called position monitoring, quality monitoring or service observing. Related terms: Calibration, Call Quality, Monitoring System.

Monitoring System. Systems that record calls in order to have a permanent record of the complete transaction and to improve the quality of call handling. While monitoring system vendors provide some unique functionality, the ability to record calls is central to all of these systems.

Recording strategies include:

- Logging: The recording of every call coming into the organization.
- Percent: A certain percent of calls are recorded to enhance the quality review process. The percent of calls can be chosen randomly or from designated types of calls.
- Scheduled: Enables the user to schedule calls to be recorded for a certain agent at a certain time.
- On demand: Enables the agent or supervisor to activate the recording feature at a moment's notice.

Organizations that implement quality monitoring/recording systems do so to improve call handling, make it more consistent and uncover ways to improve processes and systems. Payback is usually defined in terms of reductions in errors, rework, complaints, recalls, etc. Some organizations also cite a reduction in call-handling time as a result of being able to identify agents who are struggling with inefficient call-handling methods. Others have been able to reduce handling time by decreasing the amount of documentation required for a call (however, this is possible only with a logging strategy, in which every call is recorded).

Information gathered from quality monitoring/recording systems can also be used to assess the effectiveness of training and make processes more efficient. Recording systems also reduce some of the inefficiencies associated with silent monitoring. Supervisors and/or quality assurance teams no longer have to deal with issues such as starting a session in the middle of a call, losing a monitored call due to interruption, or waiting for a call to come through during a slow period. Consequently, the call center can monitor more calls with less effort and cost.

Common characteristics of these systems include:

- Feedback forms: Most systems allow the user to customize a feedback form to be used by everyone accessing the system.

- Coordinated data recording: The system records the screen activity during the call and plays it back to the reviewer, coordinated with the voice part of the call.

- Text-chat/email recording: Through the data recording capability, the system can also be used for text-chat, email and other nonphone channels.

- GUI interface for recording/playback: A user-friendly interface that enables reviewers to set up recording sessions and playback calls.

Many of the quality monitoring/recording vendors are working to increase the functionality of their systems. Some of the newer offerings include:

- Cradle-to-grave customer experience: Screen shots and voice are captured from the customer's perspective, beginning in the IVR and continuing through any and all systems until the transaction is complete.

- Integration with e-learning capabilities: Using data from the performance evaluations contained within the system, the software links with internal or external e-learning systems to identify and provide customized one-on-one training and coaching solutions.

- Integrated reporting/data mining: Some systems provide the ability to bring in data from other systems to analyze call patterns in new ways and/or create comprehensive quality reporting.

Related terms: Call Quality, Monitoring.

Most-Idle Agent. Also known as the longest-available agent. A method of distributing calls to the agent who has been idle the longest. Related terms: Least-Occupied Agent, Next Available Agent. (Vanguard)

Moves, Adds and Changes (MAC). As the term implies, MACs (pronounced "macks") are changes and/or additions to a telephone or data system.

Multi-Voting. A decision-making techique that continually reduces the number of options by conducting a series of votes. Useful when a decision has an abundance of possible solutions.

Multilingual Agents. Agents who are fluent in more than one language.

Multimedia. Combining multiple forms of media in the communication of information. A traditional phone call is "monomedia," and a Web call is "multimedia." Generically used in call centers to mean non-telephone communications (email, fax, text-chat, etc). (Vanguard)

Multimedia Queue. See Multimedia Routing and Queuing.

Multimedia Routing and Queuing. Systems and processes that handle contacts across media, including voice, text-based and Web transactions, based on business rules that define how any transaction, inquiry or problem is processed. The key differentiator is not the media, but the customer and his or her need. Business rules should be established in regard to service level and/or response time for each alternative media.

Murphy's Law. The principle of pessimists that says, if anything can go wrong, it will. Not a good perspective to live by, but worth considering when designing agent groups, routing configurations and disaster recovery plans.

Music on Hold. Background music that callers hear when they are in queue or put on hold. See American Society of Composers, Authors and Publishers.

Mute. A telephone or headset feature that enables the user to deactivate the microphone (e.g., so that he or she can cough or carry on a side conversation without the other party hearing).

Mystery Shopper. A type of monitoring in which a person acts as a customer, initiates a call to the center and monitors the skills of the agent. See Monitoring.

N-Tier Architecture. A systems architecture term that means that there can be any number of applications and databases integrated together for a business purpose. (Vanguard)

Natural Language. Technology used in speech or text recognition that identifies what is being said or requested through free-form communication No structure or specific words or phrases are required. See Speech Recognition. Related term: Directed Dialog. (Vanguard)

Needs Analysis. In a training context, a systematic and comprehensive process of assessing what training is needed in an organization. In a technology context, a needs analysis defines the technology solutions that are required to meet the organization's objectives, and how they should be configured.

Negligent Hiring. When an employer fails to use reasonable care and judgment in hiring an employee who later commits a crime during employment.

Nepotism. Showing favoritism to relatives when making HR-related decisions. Nepotism is usually not considered a favorable practice and many organizations have policies to minimize the chance for conflict of interest. However, some organizations have changed their policies to allow teams of siblings to work in their centers.

Net Present Value (NPV). A capital budgeting method, net present value is the present value of a project's future cash flow less the initial investment in the project.

Since the NPV accounts for the time value of money, it is important to understand the concept of the discount rate. The discount rate is the required rate of return that a firm must receive to justify its investments. Every large corporation, and most smaller ones, has a stated discount rate. It is easy to think of this as the competition you face for the funding you seek. If the corporation can already get, for example, a 10 percent return, why would they fund a proposed investment that would deliver less? The NPV uses this discount rate to calculate the value of an investment in today's monetary terms. This is accomplished by applying a present value interest factor (PVIF) to the cash flow of a project. An example is provided on the following page:

(continued, next page)

Initial Investment	-115,000		
Year	Cash Flow	PVIF (at 10%)	PV for Each Year
1	40,000	0.909	36,360
2	41,000	0.826	33,866
3	42,000	0.751	31,542
4	43,000	0.683	29,369
NPV			131,137

The PVIF is obtained from a table that provides the values based on the discount rate and the time period involved. Fortunately, there are ways to determine the NPV without having to resort to tables. Financial calculators can provide the information, as can spreadsheet programs. In this example, the final step is to take the NPV of the cash flows and subtract out the initial investment. When the result is a positive number, as it is in this example, the project meets the financial criteria for approval.

To use NPV to evaluate proposals, it can be converted into a profitability index (PI). The PI is the present value of cash flows divided by the initial investment outlay. A PI greater than one indicates that the project is profitable. In this example the PI would be 131,137 ÷ 115,000 = 1.14. Related terms: Discount Rate, Payback Period, Internal Rate of Return.

Net Rep. A call center agent trained to handle Internet transactions such as email, text-chat, Web callbacks, co-browsing, etc. See Agent.

Netspeak. Abbreviated spelling and colloquial phrasing employed by experienced Internet users. For example, "BTW" for "by the way" and "IMHO" for "in my humble opinion."

Network. In the call center world, the term network is typically used to describe the inter-exchange (IXC) services that route calls into a center or among several centers. The network is the "pipe" between the caller and the call center, or between call centers.

Network services include features and information, such as:

* Network routing: Although ACDs are typically the primary routing mechanism, networks also feature routing capabilities. Routing can be based on factors such as the time of day, day of week, percentage of calls to be handled at each site, area code of the calling party, DNIS, ANI or information gathered from databases via CTI. Additionally, calls can be held (queued) in the network until agents are available and then routed to the most appropriate site.

* Network reports: Provide historical or real-time information on net-

work call activity. For example, network reports can indicate how many network busies were delivered, trunk utilization, call volumes, total traffic (volume multiplied by holding times), calling numbers, etc.

- User control: Control of network features was once primarily in the hands of network providers, but in recent years, network technologies have been putting much more control in the hands of users. Today, many call centers have terminals in their facilities that directly control network features.

Networks also enable multiple sites to be networked and provide control on how calls are routed. Common types of multisite routing include:

- Percent allocation: Calls are allocated across multiple sites based on user-defined percentages.

- Call-by-call routing: Calls are routed to the optimum destination according to real-time conditions.

- Network interflow: Integrates ACD and network circuits and allows for calls to be queued simultaneously for agents groups in different sites.

Important criteria when selecting an IXC provider include the features provided, the total cost of service, redundancy of the network and how financially sound the provider is. Related terms: Call-by-Call Routing, Network Control Center, Network Interflow, Percent Allocation.

Network Computer. Sometimes referred to as a thin client. A computer, usually a PC, with limited or no disk storage, designed solely for connection to servers within a network. Applications reside on and are run within the server rather than the client. See Thin Client. (Vanguard)

Network Control Center (NCC). Also called traffic control center. In a networked call center environment, where people and equipment monitor real-time conditions across sites, change routing thresholds as necessary, and coordinate events that will impact base staffing levels. Related terms: Network, Network Management System.

Network Interface Card (NIC). A board inserted into a computer system, which enables the system to be connected to a network. Most NICs are designed for a particular type of network and protocol, although some can accommodate multiple networks.

Network Interflow. A technology used in multisite call center environments to create a more efficient distribution of calls between sites. Through integration of sites using network circuits (such as T1 circuits) and ACD software, calls routed to one site may be queued simultaneously for agent groups in remote sites. Related terms: Call-by-Call Routing, Network, Percent Allocation.

Network Management System. A management and diagnostic tool for managing a network of devices, usually via the protocol SNMP. This allows network managers to have visibility into devices like PCs, servers, data switches, routers, IP phones and voice switches for remotely diagnosing problems and troubleshooting. Related terms: Network, Network Control Center. (Vanguard)

Network Reports. Reports that provide information on network call activity (e.g., network traffic, busies and call destinations). See Network.

Network Routing. The ability to make routing decisions in the network before selecting a location to route the call. Network routing can be based on such factors as the time of day, day of week, percentage of calls to be handled at each site, area code of the calling party, DNIS or information gathered from databases via CTI. See Network. (Vanguard)

Network Service Provider (NSP). A company that provides backbone services to organizations and Internet service providers (ISPs). The NSP provides the infrastructure required for Internet connectivity, and builds, maintains and expands their infrastructure according to traffic demands. Related term: Internet Service Provider.

Next-Available Agent. A call distribution method that sends calls to the next agent who becomes available. The method seeks to maintain an equal load across skill groups or services. When there is no queue, next-available agent reverts to longest-available agent. Related terms: Least-Occupied Agent, Longest-Available Agent.

Noise-Canceling Headset. Headsets equipped with technology that reduces background noise. See Headset.

Nominal Group Technique. This weighted ranking technique is effective for determining priorities. Team members individually rank issues by importance. The issues receiving the highest votes are worked on first. Since ranking is done individually and then combined, the nominal group technique is a way to give all team members an equal voice in problem selection.

Non ACD In Calls. Inbound calls that are directed to an agent's extension rather than to a general group. These may be personal calls or calls from customers who dial the agents' extension numbers.

Non-Facility Associated Signaling (NFAS). A method of aggregating the signaling for multiple ISDN T1s or E1s onto a single D channel, thereby reducing expenses. (Vanguard)

Nonexempt Employee. Often called hourly workers, these employees are legally required to receive at least the minimum wage and may not be employed for more than 40 hours in a week without receiving at least one and one-half times their regular rate of pay for the overtime hours. Related terms: Exempt Employee, Fair Labor Standards Act.

Nonmarket Environment. See Business Environment.

Normalized Calls Per Agent. See True Calls Per Agent.

North American Numbering Plan (NANP). The NANP is the numbering plan for the Public Switched Telephone Network in the United States, Canada, Bermuda and many Caribbean nations. The areas served by the North American Numbering Plan are divided into smaller areas, each identified by a three-digit Numbering Plan Area (NPA) code, commonly called an area code. Related term: Direct-Distance Dialing.

Number Portability. A shared database among network providers that enables call centers to keep the same telephone numbers even if they change carriers.

Numbering Plan Area (NPA). See North American Numbering Plan.

NXX. In a seven digit local telephone number, NXX refers to the first three digits. N can be any number between 2 and 9, and X can be any number. Related term: North American Numbering Plan.

Object Linking and Embedding (OLE). The ability of Windows to embed an object in another object, and link the two so that when information is updated in one it is updated in the other. For example, an Excel spreadsheet can be embedded in a Word document, and the embedded document will be updated if the original Excel document is changed. In 1997, Microsoft announced that OLE was part of Active X. (Vanguard) Related term: Active X.

Object Management Group (OMG). An open membership, not-for-profit consortium that produces and maintains computer industry specifications for interoperable enterprise applications.

Object Request Broker (ORB). A middleware technology that manages communication and data exchange between objects; ORBs enable interoperability of distributed object systems by enabling objects from different vendors to communicate.

Occupancy. Also referred to as agent utilization or percent utilization. The percentage of time agents handle calls vs. wait for calls to arrive; the inverse of occupancy is idle time. For a half-hour, the typical calculation is: (Call volume x average handling time in seconds) / (number of agents x 1,800 seconds).

Occupancy is not an appropriate objective, other than as a part of high-level analysis, because it is driven by random call arrival, call type, size of the agent group, and many other variables outside the control of agents. It is important to remember that occupancy is a result of service level and random call arrival and is not a driver of service level or budgets. The service level that you are achieving at any given time will dictate the resulting occupancy rate.

In the example, a service level at 82 percent of calls answered in 20 seconds equates to an occupancy of 86 percent. If service level drops to 24 percent answer in 20 seconds, occupancy goes up to 97 percent. (Please note that these numbers refer only to this example – changes in volume and/or handle time will yield different relationships between occupancy and service level).

The terms adherence to schedule and occupancy are often incorrectly used interchangeably. They not only mean different things, they move in opposite directions. When adherence to schedule improves (goes up), occupancy goes down. Further, adherence to schedule is within the control of individuals, whereas occupancy is determined by the laws of nature, which are outside of an individual's control. Related terms: Adherence to Schedule, Idle Time, Queue Dynamics, True Calls Per Agent.

(continued, next page)

0

Avg. Talk Time: 180 sec; Avg. Work Time: 30 sec; Calls: 250		
Agents	**SL% in 20 Sec.**	**Occupancy**
30	24%	97%
31	45%	94%
32	61%	91%
33	73%	88%
34	82%	86%
35	88%	83%
36	92%	81%
37	95%	79%
38	97%	77%
39	98%	75%
40	99%	73%
41	99%	71%
42	100%	69%

Off Hook. See Busy.

Off-Peak. Periods of time other than the call center's busiest periods. Also a term to describe periods of time when long-distance carriers provide lower rates.

Off the Shelf. Hardware or software programs that are commercially available and ready for use "as is." Also refers to training programs that do not require customization.

Offered Call. Offered calls include all of the attempts callers make to reach the call center. There are three possibilities for offered calls: 1) They can get busy signals; 2) they can be answered by the system, but hang up before reaching an agent; or 3) they can be answered by an agent. Offered call reports in ACDs usually refer only to the calls that the ACD receives. Related terms: Answered Call, Handled Call, Received Call.

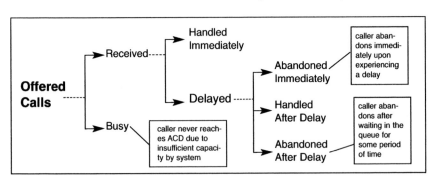

Oldest Call. See Longest Delay.

On-the-Job Training (OJT). This method of training exposes the employee to realistic job situations through observation, guided practice and while working on the job. Through constant feedback and monitoring, the employee is encouraged to take risks and add to his or her body of knowledge with each experience. As part of a formal program, the trainee actually works under the guidance of someone performing the job. Less structured programs may have a looser approach (e.g., supervisor is available to answer questions as needed). Related terms: Training, Training Strategy.

Online Analytical Processing (OLAP). A category of software reporting technologies that provide dynamic, multidimensional access to consolidated data for the purpose of extrapolating trends. Commonly used with data warehouses. (Vanguard)

Online Transaction Processing (OLTP). A category of business applications where multiple users access and update business records in real-time. OLTP is highly scalable, fast, secure and fault tolerant. In a call center, order-entry and account-inquiry applications are usually of this type. (Vanguard)

Open Database Connectivity (ODBC). A standard method of accessing databases on a variety of platforms. Defined by the SQL (Structured Query Language) Access Group. (Vanguard)

Open-Door Policy. A verbal grievance procedure where the manager is available any time an employee wants to discuss a problem. This is a way management encourages employees to discuss their problems and issues with their immediate supervisor, with the right of appeal to upper management.

Open Ticket. A customer contact (transaction) that has not been completed or resolved (closed). Related terms: First-Call Resolution, Response Time.

Operational Model. Usually refers to the organization's general structure and approach for creating value in a market. Put another way, it is the general framework for how an organization will fulfill its strategic objectives. The operational model – including the definition of customer segments, the structure of the call center, the access channels and services made available – supports the larger strategy. Related term: Strategic Business Plan.

Operator. See Attendant.

Opportunity Cost. The rate of return on the best alternative investment that is not selected. (*Barron's*)

Optical Character Recognition (OCR). Technology that reads printed text and determines what it says. Can be used with an imaging system to determine information about mail or fax items for routing and handling. Related term: Intelligent Character Recognition. (Vanguard)

Organizational Design. Professor Henry Mintzberg describes organizational design as: "The framework of jobs, positions, clusters of positions and reporting relationships among positions that are used to construct the organization." A generic but typical example of a call center organization is illustrated in the figure below.

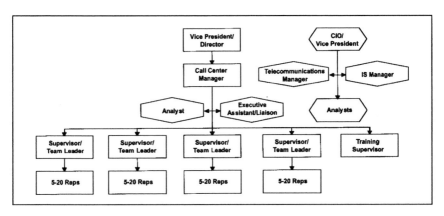

The call center is, of course, part of a larger organization. It is not necessary that call center structure reflect organizationwide structure. However, an understanding of general organizational structures can enable call center managers to better understand associated strategic and cultural implications, and the call center's role in supporting the organization's mission. Organizationwide structures can be classified as:

- Bureaucratic: Traditional, hierarchical structures
- Flat: Structures with few layers of management
- Team-oriented: Built around small groups of people working toward common objectives
- Matrix: Structures with a combination of vertical and horizontal lines of authority
- Product- or service-oriented: Structures built around the organiza-

tion's products and services

- Geographic-oriented: Structures dictated by geographical areas that the organization serves
- Customer-oriented: Structures built around customer segments

There is an infinite number of iterations and combinations of organizational structures that are possible. These classifications exist to help managers describe and define organizational structures and identify the general advantages and disadvantages of each. Related terms: Agent Group, Customer Access Strategy, Strategy.

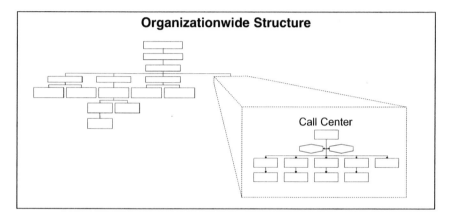

Organizationwide Structure

Orientation Program. An orientation program introduces new employees to the call center industry, organization, job and team. Key goals of orientation include reducing the anxiety and stress for new-hires, reducing the burden that the orientation process places on management and peers, and providing a favorable first impression of organization.

Out-of-Band Signaling. Passing information about a contact in a separate channel from the channel the information passes in. For example, ISDN uses out-of-band signaling to pass ANI and DNIS. (Vanguard)

Outsourcing. Contracting some or all call center services and/or technology to an outside company. The company is generally referred to as an outsourcer or service bureau.

Outsourcing relationships typically fall into one of these two types of arrangements. One possible arrangement is that the entire call center operation is outsourced. All call center staff are employed by the outsourcer and operations are typically located at the outsourcer's facility. The client directs the program objectives and measurements, while the outsourcer handles the daily management and supervision of the program. The hardware and software used may be provided by the outsourcer or, if specialized tools are needed, by the client.

Another arrangement is that some components of the client's call center operations are outsourced, while some call center functions are handled internally. Common scenarios include:

- Routine customer inquiries are outsourced; sales and customer service escalation are handled internally.
- Peak or seasonal overflow or after-hours contacts are outsourced, while the organization maintains its own call center.
- New multichannel communications are outsourced; telephone and fax communications are handled internally.
- Technical assistance is outsourced, while the organization's call center handles sales and general customer service.

Related terms: Managed Staffing Arrangement, Schedule Alternatives, Service Level Agreement.

Overflow. Calls that flow from one group or site to another. More specifically, intraflow happens when calls flow between agent groups and interflow is when calls flow out of the ACD to another site.

Overlay. See Rostered Staff Factor.

Overstaffing. A scheduling term that refers to situations when the call center has more staff than is required to handle the workload.

Overtime. Time beyond an established limit (e.g., working hours in addition to those of a regular schedule or full work week).

P&L Statement. See Income Statement.

Packet Switching. A method of transferring information across a network by passing it in small pieces (packets) of information. Typically used to transmit data (e.g., over the internet). Now being applied to voice, as well in Voice over IP applications. Related term: Voice over Internet Protocol. (Vanguard)

Page Pushing. A Web collaboration technique, enabling agents to send (push) Web pages to customers. (Vanguard)

Pareto Chart. Created by economist Vilfredo Pareto, a Pareto chart is simply a bar chart that ranks events in order of importance or frequency.

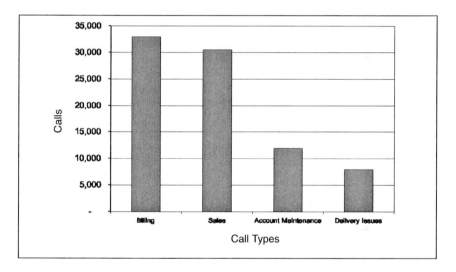

The Pareto principle dictates that you should work first on the things that will yield the biggest improvements. Example applications:
- Transactions by type
- Errors by type
- Transactions by customer demographics (e.g., age, region of country and how long they've been customers)
- Responses to customer surveys

See System of Causes.

Participative Management Style. Managers with participative styles encourage their subordinates to participate in decision-making and accept responsibility for their performance. This type of manager is better described as facilitator, coach and collaborator, as opposed to director or overseer.

Participative style management focuses on removing obstacles, providing assistance as needed and empowering the workforce. Studies have shown that subordinates of participative managers are more likely to experience intrinsic motivation (e.g., job satisfaction or sense of achievement), which has been proven to be more effective than extrinsic motivation (e.g., pay or incentives). Related term: Authoritarian Management Style.

Payback Period. A capital budgeting method that calculates the length of time required to recover an initial investment. By working in units of time, this valuation method has the advantage of being easy to understand by all involved. An example of a payback period calculation is provided below:

Initial Investment	-115,000	
Year	Cash Flow	Running Total
1	40,000	40,000
2	41,000	81,000
3	42,000	123,000
4	43,000	166,000
Payback Point	2.81 years	

In this example, the investment is recovered sometime between the end of year 2 (when $81,000 is recovered) and the end of year 3 (when $123,000 is recovered). To determine the exact payback point, the remaining investment of $34,000 that has not been recovered by the end of year 2 is divided by the total cash flow in year 3 ($42,000). The resulting number (.81) is added to the first two years to come up with the payback point of 2.81 years. In other words, this investment will be recovered in approximately two years and 10 months.

While this provides a simple and clear way to define value, it is not without flaws. First, it does not account for the time value of money. Second, and perhaps more importantly, it does not serve as a measure of profitability since the cash flows after the payback period are ignored. To highlight that last point, keep in mind that the payback period would be exactly the same if the fourth-year cash flow was zero – though the value of the investment would clearly not be equal. Related terms: Net Present Value, Internal Rate of Return.

PBX/ACD. A private branch exchange (PBX) that is equipped with ACD functionality. See Private Branch Exchange and Automatic Call Distributor.

Peaked Call Arrival. A surge of traffic beyond random variation. It is a spike within a short period of time.

There are two types of peaked traffic – the type you can plan for and incidents that are impossible to predict. If a national news program unexpectedly provides your telephone number to the viewing audience as part of its story, you will get unannounced peaked traffic. The problem is, you can't predict these events, and you're probably not willing to staff up for them just in case they happen. So staffing for unexpected peaks falls more in the categories of real-time management or disaster recovery planning.

Peaked traffic that you are expecting belongs squarely in the realm of fundamental call center planning. Forecasting, staffing and scheduling to meet a specified service level still apply. However, planning must happen at much more detailed periods of time, often in five- or 10-minute increments. For a given service level, peaked traffic requires more staff than random traffic, and agents will have a lower occupancy over a half-hour period. Related terms: Increment, Traffic Arrival.

Peer Monitoring. Call center agents monitor peers' calls and provide feedback on their performance. See Monitoring.

Penetration Rate. An outbound term that refers to the percentage of the call list that has been called.

Percent Allocation. A call routing strategy sometimes used in multisite call center environments. Calls received in the network are allocated across sites based on user-defined percentages. Related terms: Call-by-Call Routing, Network, Network Interflow.

Percent Utilization. See Occupancy.

Performance Driver. A suspect performance driver that has been validated through statistically sound analysis. See Suspect Performance Driver.

Performance Objective. Usually stated as a quantifiable goal that must be accomplished within a given set of constraints, a specified period of time, or by a given date (e.g., reduce turnover by 20 percent within one year). Generally identified with fixing a problem or pursing an opportunity. See Goal.

Performance Review. Angelo DeNisi and Ricky Griffin in *Human Resource Management* define a performance review as: "A specific and formal evaluation of an employee in order to determine the degree to which the employee is performing his or her job effectively." Performance standards are measures or levels of achievement (based on quality, quantity and/or timeliness) established by a manager for the responsibilities expressed in a job description.

Performance reviews give employees information they need to enhance their professional development and contribution to the organization. Timely reviews help to motivate employees and correct performance problems before they have a lasting effect on customer satisfaction and loyalty. Performance reviews also enable the organization to make key financial decisions regarding the value of each employee and his/her contribution to the success of the organization.

The performance review is not a monitoring or coaching session. Monitoring and coaching sessions are more frequent and focus on the particular knowledge and skills involved in handling specific customer contacts. Performance reviews should measure overall job performance based on the employee's total job responsibilities.

In many organizations, HR policy dictates the timeframe for the performance review, which may be annually based on an employee's hiring or promotion anniversary date, annually at a specified time (e.g., all employees are evaluated in December), semi-annually, quarterly or other timeframe. The annual timeframe may not be appropriate in the call center environment due to high turnover or the need to cultivate improvement opportunities for individual performance. Call center managers should work with the HR department to determine the best timeframe for performance reviews and communicate clearly to the call center staff if this timeframe differs from the rest of the organization.

Performance Target. An interim improvement point at a specific point in time, when striving to attain a new level of performance. The performance target is a "checkpoint" to reassess progress and correct the action or work plans necessary to reach the final goal. Related terms: Key Performance Indicator, Performance Objective.

Peripheral Equipment. Equipment that is not integral to, but works with, a telephone or computer system (e.g., a printer or recording device).

Permanent Placement. A staffing term, related to using a staffing agency for the hiring process. The staffing agency handles all advertising and publicity and screens candidates using basic criteria (e.g., phone screen, testing). They may also handle other administrative tasks for the contracting party (e.g., reference or background checks, security clearance process). Typically, the call center handles face-to-face interviews and hiring decisions. A one-time fee is paid to the staffing agency, either at the time of hire or after a waiting period.

Personal Computer (PC). A computer designed for use by one person at a time. Personal computers do not need to share the processing, disk, storage or printer resources of another computer (although they can through a network). IBM compatible PCs and Apple Macintoshes are common examples of personal computers.

Personal Digital Assistant (PDA). A small, lightweight "palmtop" computer often used for personal organization tasks (e.g., calendar, database, calculator and note-taking functions) and communications (e.g., email, wireless Internet access and, in some cases, wireless telephone). Recent models offer multimedia features (e.g., cameras, music storage and playback, and video storage and playback). Most PDAs use flash memory instead of disk drives, and rely on pens or other pointing devices rather than a keyboard or mouse.

Pilot Program. An experimental program to assess viability. Designed to determine whether a technology, process or program being considered is feasible, and to provide input on how it should be modified. Often on a smaller scale than subsequent programs that are implemented.

Pinpoint Survey. A survey that is targeted for only one customer segment or set of issues. See Customer Survey.

Planning Culture. A call center workforce management philosophy that relies heavily on preparation in the utilization of staff resources. A call center that practices a planning culture typically spends more time planning for tomorrow than explaining yesterday. Related term: Chaos Mentality.

Poisson. A formula sometimes used for calculating trunks. Assumes that if callers get busy signals, they keep trying until they successfully get through. Since some callers won't keep retrying, Poisson can overestimate trunks required. Related terms: Erlang B, Retrial Tables, Trunk Load.

Pooled Agent Group. See Agent Group.

Pooling Principle. The powerful pooling principle states: Any movement in the direction of consolidation of resources will result in improved traffic-carrying efficiency. Conversely, any movement away from consolidation of resources will result in reduced traffic-carrying efficiency. As illustrated in the table, one group of 15 agents can do the work of two groups of nine agents – all other things equal.

Calls in 1/2 Hour	Service Level	Agents Required	Occupancy	Avg. Calls Per Agent
50	80/20	9	65%	5.6
100	80/20	15	78%	6.7
500	80/20	65	90%	7.7
1000	80/20	124	94%	8.1

Assumption: Calls last an average 3.5 minutes.

A common call center application is that if you take several small, specialized agent groups, effectively cross train them and put them into a single group, you'll have a more efficient environment (assuming all other things are equal). Related terms: Agent Group, Queue Dynamics, Skills-Based Routing.

Position Monitoring. See Monitoring.

Post-Call Processing (PCP). See After-Call Work.

Post Office Protocol 3 (POP 3). A standard for retrieving email, which is used by many email systems. (Vanguard)

Predictive Dialer. See Dialer.

Pregnancy Discrimination Act (U.S.). The Pregnancy Discrimination Act of 1978 requires that employers treat a pregnant job applicant or employee the same as they would any employee with a medical condition.

Present Value Interest Factor (PVIF). See Net Present Value.

Preview Dialer. See Dialer.

Primary Carrier. The primary long-distance carrier the customer chooses to carry long-distance traffic. The carrier that handles long-distance traffic when the customer dials "1" plus the area code and number.

Primary Rate Interface (PRI). One of two levels of ISDN service. In North America, PRI typically provides 23 bearer channels for voice and data and one channel for signaling information (commonly expressed as

23B+D). In Europe, PRI typically provides 30 bearer lines (30B+D).
Related terms: Basic Rate Interface, Integrated Services Digital Network.

Priority Queuing Application. Programming that recognizes and
"bumps" higher-value customers up in the queue to ensure that they
receive the most efficient service possible.

Privacy. The expectation that confidential or personal information dis-
closed in a private setting will not be made public. Call center managers
should develop policies that address privacy-related issues. Important
aspects of this responsibility include:

- Communicate your policy regarding privacy. Employees and call
  center managers need to have a clear, mutual understanding of what
  each may and may not do. This should be part of every orientation
  program, in the employee handbook and disseminated to all employees.

- Make employees aware of any electronic surveillance devices that are
  being used. Generally, undisclosed monitoring should be avoided
  and separate, unmonitored phone lines should be made available for
  personal phone calls.

Private Automatic Branch Exchange (PABX). See Private Branch
Exchange.

Private Branch Exchange (PBX). Also called private automatic branch
exchange (PABX). A telephone system located at the call center's site that
handles incoming and outgoing calls. ACD software can provide PBXs
with ACD functionality. Many refer to a PBX as a "switch."

Private Network. A network made up of circuits for the exclusive use
of an organization or group of affiliated organizations. Can be regional,
national or international in scope and are common in large organizations.

Process. A system of causes. See System of Causes.

Product-Oriented Organizational Design. See Organizational
Design.

Products or Services Per Customer. A performance measure. A sim-
pler variation of sales per customer, products or services per customer can
be a measure of cross-selling effectiveness. In general, increases in the
average number of products or services per customer are desirable and
should increase customer value. Related term: Sales Per Customer.

Profit-and-Loss Statement. See Income Statement.

Profit Center. An accounting term that refers to a department or function in the organization that generates profit. While call centers that are considered profit centers keep an eye on expenses, they also track value activities in the call center.

The attention placed on value drives different activities than those in a cost center. For example, cost centers are often focused on average handle time and doing whatever it takes to keep this as low as possible. In a profit center, the organization will look for ways to increase value during the call. This often leads to efforts to promote cross-sell opportunities or gather important customer data. The extra investment in time increases talk time and staffing requirements, but is considered to be a worthwhile because the value generated by these extra steps covers the investment. Related term: Cost Center.

Profitability Index (PI). See Net Present Value.

Progressive Dialer. See Dialer.

Project Management. The process of planning, managing and controlling the course and development of a project or undertaking (e.g., implementing a new ACD or opening a new call center). Key project management terms include:

- Scope: The boundaries of the project, meaning a statement of what is and is not part of the project. Also, "scope creep" is when a project grows beyond what was originally approved, often because the scope was not clearly defined at the outset.

- Project plan (also known as work breakdown structure, or WBS): Listing of all tasks required to complete the project showing (for each task) start date, completion date, resources required, the person responsible for each task and a task number.

- Gantt chart: Visual representation of the project plan, using bars extending to the right of each task representing the amount of time the task requires. Sophisticated Gantt charts use arrows and symbols to indicate task dependencies, milestones, etc.

- Milestone: Measurable point of progress in the project plan. The milestone is listed in the project plan along with the tasks, but is present really as a marker that either has or has not been achieved. For example, "Collect responses to request for proposal."

- Deliverables: Completed units of work with tangible results. For example, a report could be a deliverable, as could a software module.

- Dependency: Relationship between tasks that makes planning for one task dependent upon planning for the other. For example, "determine number of trunks needed" must be completed before "place order for trunks."

- Critical path: The sequence of tasks upon which the project completion date depends. In other words, a change in the duration of any these tasks will change the project's completion date, due to dependencies among the tasks on the critical path. Tasks that are not on the critical path can be delayed without affecting the project end date.

- Owner: Person accountable for completion of a task.

- Sponsor/champion: Person in the organization with the authority and/or funds to make the project happen, or who advocates for the project to the organization's decision makers.

Prompted Digits. See Caller-Entered Digits.

Protected Class. A group of people who have suffered past discrimination and have been given special protection by the judicial system. Defined and designated in Title VII of the Civil Rights Act of 1964 (U.S.).

Psychographics. The use of demographics to study and measure customer lifestyles, opinions, and preferences. Used for marketing purposes.

Public Service Commission (PSC). Also called public utility commission in some states in the United States. The agency in each state that regulates communications, power and other public utility services.

Public-Switched Network (PSN). See Public-Switched Telephone Network.

Public Switched Telephone Network (PSTN). The public telephone network that provides the capability of interconnecting any home or office with any other.

Public Utility Commission (PUC). See Public Service Commission.

Qualitative Analysis. Analysis that interprets descriptive data, and is usually expressed as text. Related term: Quantitative Analysis.

Quality Monitoring. See Monitoring

Quality Monitoring System. See Monitoring System.

Quality of Service (QOS). A data-networking management method to provide different packets different priorities when there is congestion. For call centers, QOS is critical for VoIP applications. Packets are tagged for QOS with a Class-of-Service header. (Vanguard)

Quantitative Analysis. Analysis that focuses on numerical, mathematical or statistical data. Related term: Qualitative Analysis.

Quantitative Forecasting. Using statistical techniques to forecast future events. The major categories of quantitative forecasting include time series and explanatory approaches. Time-series techniques use past trends to forecast future events. Explanatory techniques attempt to reveal linkages between two or more variables. Related terms: Forecasting Methodologies, Judgmental Forecasting.

Queue. Queue literally means "line of waiting people." (Note: Queue can also mean agent group – see Agent Group.) Queues are a fact of life in most incoming call centers because answering every call immediately would require as many agents as callers who need service at any given time. That is impractical for most organizations (although most emergency services centers do staff at levels that enable immediate answer much of the time).

The difference between an incoming call center and the lines at the grocery store is that callers often don't know where they are in queue and the progress they are making. In other words, callers usually encounter an invisible queue.

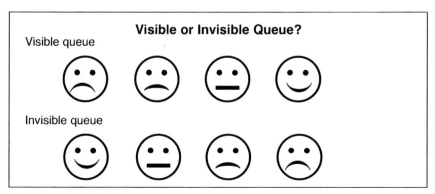

Visible or Invisible Queue?

Visible queue

Invisible queue

The top row of faces in the illustration represents the psychology of customers when they can "see" the queue – a visible queue. Few would choose to wait in line, so as they enter the queue they are represented by the first face. As they move forward, the subsequent faces illustrate their progress. The second row of faces represents a setting where customers are ignorant of the queue they are entering. Expectations are initially high, but as time passes, they become frustrated.

Many ACD systems have the ability to announce expected wait times to callers, by using predictive wait messaging. With this feature, the ACD is programmed to analyze real-time variables, make predictions and announce expected wait times to callers as they arrive. These systems provide fairly accurate predictions in reasonably straightforward environments, especially in large agent groups. They are far less accurate when complex, contingency-based routing is in place or in small agent groups.

If wait times are long, providing estimated wait times may cause some callers to hang up soon after reaching the center. But those who stay in queue are more likely to remain until they get an answer. Many call center managers keep a diligent eye on how many callers abandon. But *when* callers abandon is an important consideration as well. If they are abandoning early because they are making an informed choice, that's a very different scenario than waiting for a lengthy period only to abandon in frustration. Related terms: Caller Tolerance, Invisible Queue, Visible Queue.

Queue Display. See Readerboard.

Queue Dynamics. Queue dynamics refer to how queues behave. To illustrate queue dynamics, consider an example of a half-hour increment using the classic queuing formula, Erlang C. (This illustration is based on the Erlang C program QueueView, developed by Incoming Calls Management Institute. Similar Erlang C calculators are available from ACD vendors and other software companies.)

	SL%			Trunk Load
Agents	in 20 Sec.	ASA	Occ.	(in hours)
30	24%	208.7	97%	54.0
31	45%	74.7	94%	35.4
32	61%	37.6	91%	30.2
33	73%	21.3	88%	28.0
34	82%	12.7	86%	26.8
35	88%	7.8	83%	26.1
36	92%	4.9	81%	25.7
37	95%	3.1	79%	25.4
38	97%	1.9	77%	25.3
39	98%	1.2	75%	25.2
40	99%	0.7	73%	25.1
41	99%	0.5	71%	25.1
42	100%	0.3	69%	25.0

Avg. Talk Time: 180 sec; Avg. Work Time: 30 sec; Calls: 250

Source: ICMI QueueView: A Staffing Calculator

Erlang C requires four variables:

- Average talk time, in seconds: Input the projected average for the future half-hour you are analyzing.

- Average after-call work, in seconds: Input the projected average for the future half-hour you are analyzing.

- Number of calls: Input the projected volume for the future half-hour you are analyzing.

- Service level objective in seconds: If your service level objective is to answer 90 percent of calls in 20 seconds, input 20 seconds. If it's 80 percent in 15 seconds, plug in 15 seconds. In other words, the formula needs the Y seconds in the service level definition, "X percent of calls answered in Y seconds."

Here's what the column headings stand for:

- Agents: Number of agents required to be on the phones, plugged in and available to handle calls. In this case, 34 agents will achieve a service level of 82 percent answered in 20 seconds.

- SL: The percentage of calls that will be answered in the number of seconds you specify.

- ASA (average speed of answer): ASA is the average delay of all calls, including the ones that aren't delayed at all. With 34 agents handling calls, ASA will be 13 seconds.

- OCC (percent agent occupancy): The percentage of time agents will spend handling calls, including talk time and after-call work. The balance of time, they are available and waiting for calls. In the example, occupancy will be 86 percent.

- TKLD: This column is the hours (erlangs) of trunk traffic, which is the product of (talk time plus average speed of answer) multiplied by number of calls in an hour. Since Erlang B and other alternatives used for calculating trunks often require input in hours, these numbers can be readily used as they are. The actual traffic carried by trunks in a half-hour will, in each row, be half of what is given.

Notice some of the dynamics that become evident from these calculations:

- The more agents you have handling calls, the higher service level will be.

- The more agents you have handling calls, the lower trunk load will be.

- The more agents you have handling calls, the lower occupancy will be.

Because of random call arrival, different callers can experience very different queue times, even if they are part of the same set of data measured by service level, ASA and other reports. A good question to ask for any service level is, "What happens to the calls that don't get answered in Y seconds?" Some Erlang C and computer simulation programs will calculate the answers to that and other questions. For a service level of 80 percent answered in 20 seconds, about 30 percent of callers end up in queue, the longest wait will be around three minutes, and average speed of answer will be around 10 to 15 seconds.

As illustrated in the table, with 34 agents service level will be 82 percent of calls answered in 20 seconds. Sixty-five callers will wait five seconds or longer. In the next five seconds, seven of those callers reach agents, so only 58 callers are waiting 10 seconds or longer. In the next five seconds, six more callers will reach agents, leaving only 52 callers waiting 15 seconds or more. At this service level, one caller is still waiting at three minutes.

Note two important implications of the principle of delay:

1. Because of random call arrival, different callers have different experiences even though they called during the same half-hour, and even though the call center may be hitting its target service level.

2. Some call centers attempt to set two service levels for the same queue, e.g., to handle 80 percent of calls in 20 seconds and the rest

within 60 seconds. Obviously, that is not possible; 80/20 and 100/60 are distinctly different service levels.

Delay Module
ERLANG C FOR INCOMING CALL CENTERS BY ICMI, INC.
TALK TIME IN SECONDS = **180**
AFTER-CALL WORK IN SECONDS = **30**
CALLS PER HALF-HOUR = **250**
SERVICE LEVEL OBJECTIVE IN SECONDS = **20**

I<========= Number of callers waiting longer than x seconds =========>I

Agents	SL%	5	10	15	20	30	40	50	60	90	120	180	240
30	24	203	199	195	191	184	177	170	163	145	129	101	80
31	45	156	149	143	137	126	115	105	97	74	57	34	20
32	61	118	111	104	97	85	74	65	56	38	25	11	5
33	73	89	81	74	67	56	47	39	32	19	11	4	1
34	82	65	58	52	46	37	29	23	18	9	5	1	0
35	88	47	41	36	31	24	18	14	10	4	2	0	0
36	92	34	29	24	21	15	11	8	6	2	1	0	0
37	95	24	20	16	14	9	6	4	3	1	0	0	0
38	97	16	13	11	9	6	4	2	2	0	0	0	0
39	98	11	9	7	5	3	2	1	1	0	0	0	0
40	99	7	6	4	3	2	1	1	0	0	0	0	0
41	99	5	4	3	2	1	1	0	0	0	0	0	0
42	100	3	2	2	1	1	0	0	0	0	0	0	0

Source: ICMI QueueView: A Staffing Calculator

Related terms: Agent Group, Average Speed of Answer, Occupancy, Service Level, Trunk Load.

Queue Time. See Delay.

Quick Disconnect. A modular connection that enables a headset to quickly be disconnected from a telephone set. See Headset.

Random Availability. The normal, random variation in the availability of agents due to variations in talk time, after-call work and call arrival. Related terms: Occupancy, Queue Dynamics.

Random Call Arrival. The normal, random variation in how incoming calls arrive. See Traffic Arrival.

Readerboard. Also called display board, queue display, wallboard or electronic display. A visual display, usually mounted on the wall or ceiling of a call center, which provides real-time and historical information on queue conditions, agent status and call center performance. It can also display user-entered messages (e.g., "Happy Birthday, Grace!").

Real-Time Adherence. See Adherence to Schedule.

Real-Time Adherence Software. A function of workforce management software that tracks how closely agents conform to their schedules. See Adherence to Schedule.

Real-Time Management. Making adjustments to staffing and thresholds in the systems and network in response to current queue conditions. To achieve your service level and response time objectives in real-time, you need to make appropriate tactical adjustments as conditions change. Real-time adjustments may include:

- Ensure everyone available is taking a call
- Assist people who are stuck in talk time or after-call work
- Postpone flexible work
- Record appropriate system announcements
- Bring in secondary groups
- Adjust overflow or network parameters
- Reassign agents to groups that need help
- Adjust the placement of delay announcements
- Use supervisors "wisely"
- Bring in agents who are on call
- Send calls to outsourcers
- Mobilize the "swat team" (help from other departments)
- Adjust call routing priorities
- Take messages for callback
- Generate controlled busy signals

An important principle in effective real-time management is to outline a workable escalation plan that is in place before a crisis. Most call centers use a tiered approach:

- Level 1: The first level of action involves routine, common sense adjustments that enable you to get the calls answered. Agent status becomes the focus, and many use a variation of the time-honored phrase: "Everybody take a call!" This is generally directed toward people on the floor who are not currently handling calls. It can also be for agents stuck in after-call work.

  At this level, agents make routine adjustments to work priorities. Flexible tasks are postponed. If you have a secondary group handling correspondence, outbound calls or data-entry, they can be temporarily assigned to the inbound traffic. You might also overflow calls to agents in other groups (who are trained to handle the calls).

- Level 2 and beyond: If the workload still outpaces the staff required to handle it, the call center can move on to more involved real-time alternatives. For example, it may be feasible to reassign agents from one group to another. Or, you might change call-routing thresholds between groups or sites. Other Level 2 tactics include calling in a "swat team," bringing in agents who are on reserve, routing some calls to established outsourcers, adjusting the placement of delay announcements and generating controlled busy signals.

In short, establishing an effective escalation plan involves:

- Identifying feasible real-time tactics (ahead of time)
- Determining the conditions in which each should be implemented (ahead of time)
- Monitoring conditions (real-time)
- Deciding on adjustments necessary (real-time)
- Coordinating and communicating changes to all involved (real-time)
- Implementing the tactics (real-time)
- Assessing how well the escalation plan worked (after-the-fact)

Related terms: Chaos Mentality, Queue Dynamics, Real-Time Report, Service Level.

Real-Time Report. Information on current conditions. Some real-time information is real-time in the strictest sense (e.g., calls in queue and current longest wait). Some real-time reports require some history (i.e., the last x calls or x minutes) in order to make a calculation (e.g., service level and average speed of answer). Related terms: Historical Report, Screen Refresh.

Real-Time Threshold. A marker that is identified in advance (e.g., number of calls in queue, longest in queue, etc.) that automatically initiates a certain response in a call center. For example, at a given time, a call center may not react to a queue unless it reaches 25 calls or more.

Received Call. A call detected and seized by a trunk. Received calls will either abandon or be answered by an agent. Related terms: Answered Call, Handled Call, Offered Call.

Receptionist. See Attendant.

Record. An entry in a database.

Record and Review Monitoring. See Monitoring.

Recorded Announcement. A general reference to announcements callers hear while waiting in queue. Recorded announcements may remind callers to have certain information ready for the call, include general information about products or services, or provide alternative contact alternatives (e.g., "Visit our Web site at..."), etc. See Delay Announcement.

Recorded Announcement Device. A system component that enables recording, playback and control of delay and informational announcements, as well as music and/or other content played while callers are in queue or on hold. Related terms: Recorded Announcement, Delay Announcement.

Recorded Announcement Route (RAN). See Delay Announcement.

Recruiting. The process of developing a pool of qualified candidates who are interested in working for your call center. Recruiting should also provide realistic job previews to candidates. Sources of new candidates may come from referrals from current employees, former employees, customers, competitors, schools and local colleges, employment agencies and others.

Just as there are many sources of candidates, there are many related methods of recruiting. Examples include:

- Internal job postings; e.g., through an Intranet
- Recommendations by a team leader, supervisor or manager
- Union hall
- The organization's Web site
- Career/job sites on the Internet
- Employment agencies

- Print advertisements; e.g., local and national papers, professional journals, trade magazines, inserts in catalogs and sales flyers
- Mall handouts
- Job fairs

Redial. Dialing a telephone number again after a failed attempt.

Redirection Message. See Delay Announcement.

Reduced Instruction Set Computing (RISC). A microprocessor designed to speed computer performance. RISC chips rapidly and efficiently process a relatively small set of instructions that comprise most of the instructions a computer must execute. RISC architecture optimizes these instructions so that they can be carried out very rapidly.

Redundancy. When a component or system is backed up by or shares the load with another component or system. Redundant systems ensure that, if there is a component failure, another component or system will keep the system going. See Disaster Recovery Plan.

Reengineering. A term popularized by management consultant Michael Hammer. Refers to fundamentally redesigning processes to improve efficiency and service.

Regional Bell Operating Company (RBOC). The individual companies that were created when the old Bell System was broken up into seven "baby bells." Only a few remain, due to mergers and acquisitions.

Regression Analysis. Statistical analysis of the degree to which an independent variable affects a dependent variable. For example, regression analysis could determine the impact of average handling time on average sales, or the degree to which experience level impacts contact quality scores.

Remote Agent. A fully integrated call center agent residing at home or other remote location. Requires both telephony and data connectivity from a main site to the agent's location, and the same features and functions available to agents on site. Also called home agent and telecommuter. Related term: Telecommuting. (Vanguard)

Remote Office. A group of agents (or a single agent working at a site separate from the main call center) that use the same technology infrastructure (voice switch, applications and other elements) as the main call center. The agent(s) could be located in a branch office or another center. Related term: Satellite Office. (Vanguard)

Replacement Cost. The current purchase price of an asset used to replace an existing asset. (*Barron's*)

Request for Information (RFI). A document sent to potential solutions providers that describes project requirements in high-level, generic terms. RFIs are generally issued to a broad range of possible vendors, in order to become aware of the breadth and scope of possible solutions. See Request for Proposal.

Request for Proposal (RFP). A document sent to potential solutions providers that describes project requirements in focused, specific terms. RFPs are generally issued to fewer vendors than RFIs, and more specifically outline important criteria for potential solutions. See Request for Information.

Request for Quote (RFQ). An RFQ can be part of a Request for Information or Request for Proposal, or issued separately, and results in a price for a solution. Related terms: Request for Information, Request for Proposal.

Resolution. A measure of when the problem or issue is actually resolved. Used in environments where the call center's initial response may not fully resolve the issue. For example, in a technical support environment additional research after the call may be necessary. The problem is "resolved" when the matter is handled to completion and the "trouble ticket" is closed. See Response Time.

Resource Reservation Protocol (RSVP). A network-control protocol that enables Internet applications to use differing qualities of service (QOS) for their data flows. Applications such as videoconferencing or IP telephony require timely data delivery, but reliable data delivery is not as important. Traditional batch or interactive applications require reliable data delivery, but do not necessarily depend on timely delivery. Accordingly, RSVP is intended to provide IP networks with the capability to support different performance requirements for different types of applications.

Response Time. Defined as "100 percent of contacts handled within N days/hours/minutes" (e.g., all email will be handled within 240 minutes or all faxes will be responded to within 24 hours). It is the preferred objective for contacts that do not have to be handled when they arrive. (See Service Level.)

There are two types of response time:

- Scheduled response time, like a dry-cleaning service, is geared around blocks of time. For example, you may commit to handle all messages received up to noon by 5 p.m., and to respond to messages received between noon and 5 p.m. by 10 a.m. the next morning.

- Rolling response time is hinged on the specific times each message arrives. For example, if you establish a four-hour response time, a customer who sends a message at 9:03 a.m. should get a response by 1:03 p.m., and one who sends a message at 9:12 a.m. should receive a response by 1:12 p.m.

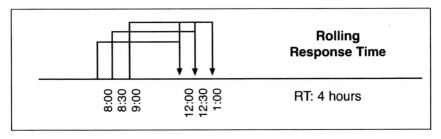

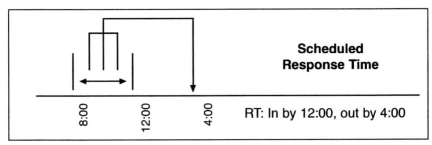

In the context of handling transactions that do not have to be handled immediately, there are three types of response:

- Automated reply: This is a system-generated response that automatically sends a reply to the customer acknowledging that the email they sent was received and informing them of when to expect a response. This establishes appropriate expectations and minimizes telephone calls or other additional contacts inquiring about the status of the original message.

- Response: This refers to the response the customer receives when the transaction is actually handled by the call center. The time that elapses between the customer's original message and the call center's response is measured as response time.

- Resolution: This is a measure of when the problem or issue is actually resolved and is used in environments where the call center's initial response may not fully resolve the issue. For example, in a technical support environment additional research after the contact may be necessary. The problem is "resolved" when the matter is handled to completion and the "trouble ticket" is closed.

Today, many call centers are establishing straightforward, 24-hour scheduled response time objectives, but some in more competitive environments are targeting rolling response times of four hours or even one hour or less. In fact, some call centers are treating email messages like telephone calls, and handling them as they arrive or soon thereafter, in which case, service level rather than response time objectives apply. The following table illustrates typical objectives:

Type of Transaction	Low end of range	High end of range
Customer email	48 to 72 hours	Less than one hour
Fax	Three days	Three hours
Voicemail	Next day	Within one hour
Letter by mail	One week	Same day

* from industry surveys

When establishing and assessing either service level or response time objectives, remember that it's not just how high your overall stated objectives are, but how consistently you hit them throughout the day. Related Definitions: Response Time Calculation, Service Level, Service Level Calculations.

Response Time Calculation. Calculating staff requirements for a workload that does not have to be handled at the time it arrives is generally based on the centuries-old "units-of-output" approach.

Here's the logic: If you get 60 messages that have an average handling time of four minutes, that's four hours of workload. One agent working non-stop could handle the load in four hours. If you need to complete the transactions within two hours, you will need a minimum of two agents working over a period of two hours. So, as with service level and inbound telephone calls, the email workload and response time objective dictate staff requirements. Accordingly, the basic formula for calculating the minimum staff required is:

(continued, next page)

Basic Formula

$$\frac{\text{Volume}}{(\text{RT} \div \text{AHT})} = \text{Agents}$$

Volume = Volume for forecast increment (e.g., volume per hour)
RT = Response time
AHT = Average handling time

Volume is the quantity of transactions you must handle, AHT is the average amount of time it takes agents to handle the transactions (the equivalent of average talk time and average after-call work for inbound telephone calls), and response time is the time you have to respond to customers after receiving their messages. Using the formula, you could handle the 60 messages previously mentioned in two hours with $60 \div (120 \div 4) = 2$ agents.

There are several things to keep in mind:

- There are many ways you can slice and dice base staff schedules to achieve your objectives. In fact, in the example, you could have 60 agents rush in and handle all 60 transactions just before the promised response time and still meet your objective. What you are really doing is looking for an efficient way to distribute the workload across your schedules within the promised response time.

- When response time objectives are less than an hour, traffic engineers generally recommend using Erlang C or computer simulation to calculate base staff. This would be a queuing and service level scenario, like inbound telephone calls.

- An "efficiency factor" acknowledges that agents cannot handle one transaction after another with no "breathing" time in between. For example, if you want to build in an efficiency factor with a ceiling of 90 percent, divide base staff calculations by .9 to calculate if additional agents are required.

- Breaks, absenteeism and other activities that keep agents from the work need to be added to base staff calculations through a rostered staff factor.

This is a basic approach, and does not account for variables such as work carried over from previous intervals. As with service level calculations, an appropriate staffing calculator or scheduling system can take much of the guesswork out of response time variables. See Response Time.

Responsibility Charting. Involves the creation of a matrix in which each team member is assigned a role in the decision-making process. For example, some team members are responsible for making the decision while others simply provide input.

Retained Earnings. See Statement of Retained Earnings.

Retention. The opposite of turnover; keeping employees in the call center. Solid retention strategies start with sound hiring practices. Taking time to select the right people for positions is the best investment a call center can make to avoid turnover. In addition to effective hiring practices, the following factors have a significant impact on the success of retention programs:

- The leadership in the call center and organization
- The call center environment
- Kinds of incentives and rewards offered
- Public recognition
- Perception of internal and external compensation equity
- Perception employees have of the environment of which they are a part

See Turnover.

Retrial. Also called redial. When a person tries again to complete a call, after encountering a busy signal.

Retrial Tables. Sometimes used to calculate trunks and other system resources required. They assume that some callers will make additional attempts to reach the call center if they get busy signals. Related terms: Erlang B, Poisson.

Return on Assets (ROA). A ratio that divides net income (or earnings) by average total assets. The resulting percentage indicates how much income has been generated from each dollar of the organization's assets.

Return on Investment (ROI). Strictly speaking, this is the net income divided by total assets. It is important to note that ROI in the strictest sense is not a capital budgeting method, but is instead a method of evaluating financial statements that generates a ratio of net income after taxes to total assets. In call center use, however, ROI has come to define a generic method of estimating the value of an investment. In this manner, the ROI of a project is typically calculated as the percentage return over the first year of the investment.

Too often, ROI calculations are overly simplistic. For example, a workforce management system vendor may suggest that the system will generate a reduction in staffing expenses of $15,000 a month for the first year, or $180,000 in total for the year. This number will likely be compared to the initial outlay of $60,000, leading to an ROI estimate of 300 percent ($180,000 ÷ $60,000). However, this simple analysis does not account for all project costs, or the time value of money, and therefore does not present an accurate representation of the value of the project. In short, credible ROI calculations will consider all relevant factors. Related terms: Internal Rate of Return, Net Present Value, Payback Period.

Return on Sales (ROS). A calculation that divides net income by sales to indicate if the return on sales is high enough. A low return on sales could indicate insufficient price mark-up to cover expenses.

Revenue. In a call center context, revenue often refers to a measure of the revenues attributed to call center services. Revenue information requires data from several reports/sources; e.g., sales reports, total orders, CRM system reports, etc. In other words, any report that indicates revenue generated by the call center. Results are often correlated with other variables such as call center costs, market conditions and revenues through other channels of contact (e.g., retail or direct sales force) to gauge the call center's impact on the organization's profits. Related term: Incremental Revenue Analysis.

Revenue Per Customer. See Sales Per Customer.

Ring Delay. Also called delay before answer. An ACD feature that enables the system to adjust the number of rings before the system automatically answers a call.

Risk. In a financial context, risk is the degree of uncertainty associated with the outcome of a project or investment. See Technology Adoption Lifecycle.

Rolling Response Time. See Response Time.

Root Cause. A primary cause of a problem or outcome. See System of Causes.

Rostered Staff Factor (RSF). Alternatively called overlay, shrink factor or shrinkage. RSF is a numerical factor that leads to the minimum staff needed on schedule over and above base staff required to achieve your service level and response time objectives. It is calculated after base staffing is determined and before schedules are organized, and accounts for things like breaks, absenteeism and ongoing training.

Calculating RSF is a form of forecasting. The major assumption is that the proportion of staff off the phones will be similar to what is happening now. In other words, if one person is on break in a group of 10, 10 people will be on break in a group of 100. An illustration of how to calculate RSF is shown in the following table.

The mechanics include five steps:

Rostered Staff Factor (Shrinkage) Calculations

	Base Staff Phone	Required Email	Absent	Break	Training	On Schedule	Rostered Staff Factor
08:00-08:30	18	4	2	0	0	24	1.09
08:30-09:00	20	4	2	0	4	30	1.25
09:00-09:30	20	4	2	0	4	30	1.25
09:30-10:00	25	5	2	3	4	39	1.3
10:00-10:30	25	5	2	3	4	39	1.3
10:30-11:00	31	5	2	3	4	45	1.25

$$\text{Rostered Staff Factor} = \frac{\text{On Schedule}}{\text{Base Staff Required}}$$

1. Enter the base staff required by half-hour: What base staff includes will depend on the structure of your groups. If you have separate agent groups for transactions that must be handled when they arrive and transactions that can be handled at a later time, the base staff entered represents one of those groups. You will need shrinkage calculations for each group. On the other hand, if you set up groups that handle both types of transactions, base staff is first calculated for both types of work separately and then added together. You would then calculate the shrink factor for the combined group.

2. Identify the things that routinely keep agents from the workload: The next three columns reflect the numbers of staff absent, on break and in training, as they now occur. These categories are just examples, and you can include research, outbound calls (those that are not part of talk time or after-call work) and other activities. You may also want to further subdivide the categories. For example, absenteeism can be divided into planned absenteeism, such as vacations, and unplanned absenteeism, such as sick leave.

3. Add base staff to the number of agents who will be away from the workload, for each half-hour: The "on-schedule" column is the sum of the entries in previous columns, by half-hour.

4. Calculate RSF: The last column is derived by dividing the staff required on schedule by base staff required, for each half-hour. The proportions are the mechanism you will use to project future shrinkage.

5. Use the factors when organizing future schedules: The result of these calculations is a set of factors reflecting expected shrinkage by half-hour. You multiply them against the base staff you will need when assembling future schedules. For example, if you are putting together a schedule for two weeks from now, and you need 32 base staff between 8:30 and 9:00, you will need to schedule 40 agents (32 x 1.25) for that half-hour – plus any staff required to be working on projects, in meetings or anything else not included in the shrinkage calculation.

While breaks and absenteeism should almost always be included in shrink factor calculations, other activities require some analysis and judgment. For example, if training schedules frequently change and/or require differing proportions of staff, keep training information out of shrinkage calculations and, instead, factor it into schedules on a case-by-case basis.

In many call centers, shrink factor falls between 1.1 and 1.4 throughout the day, meaning that a minimum of 10 percent to 40 percent additional staff are required on schedule over those handling the workload. However, if activities not related to the workload are significant, shrink factor can be as high as 2.0, meaning that you'll need to schedule two people for each agent required. This is fairly common in some help desks that have extensive off-line research. Related term: Base Staff.

Round-Robin Distribution. A method of distributing calls to agents according to a predetermined list. Related terms: Next-Available Agent, Least-Occupied Agent, Longest-Waiting Agent.

Router. A data-networking device that connects LANs through a WAN. It contains sophisticated algorithms for calculating the best paths between two end devices. (Vanguard)

Sales Force Automation (SFA). The use of computer and communications systems to support and boost the productivity of salespeople. More specifically, SFA is a class of business applications designed to automate the marketing and sales process. Historically, they were limited to such areas as "opportunity management" and "interactive selling." Today, the term usually refers to any technology-enabled sales tools and often includes contact and customer relationship management. Related term: Customer Relationship Management. (Vanguard)

Sales Per Customer. A performance measure that can also be referred to as revenue per customer. In a sales-oriented call center (as opposed to a service center), sales results will likely already be tracked closely. A customer-centric view of sales, however, may not be feasible prior to implementing a unified customer relationship management initiative. Sales per customer should reflect all products and services the customer has with the organization (across all departments and product lines). Attention to the relationship each customer has with the organization is usually expected to increase the amount of sales per customer (in a profit-making organization). Related term: Products or Services Per Customer.

Sampling. The process of using a portion of the total survey population to gauge the probable response of the entire population. In general, sampling is done randomly to allow the results to be representative of the total population. Related term: Customer Survey.

Satellite Office. A call center location that operates using a cabinet or carrier of a switch from a main location. Used to extend one switch to another site to operate virtually without purchasing a second switch. Related term: Remote Office. (Vanguard)

Scatter Diagram. A quality tool that assesses the strength of the relationship between two variables. Is used to test and document possible cause-and-effect.

If there is positive correlation between the two variables, dots will appear as an upward slope. If there is a negative correlation, the dots will appear as a downward slope. The closer the pattern of dots is to a straight line, the stronger the correlation is between the two variables.

(continued, next page)

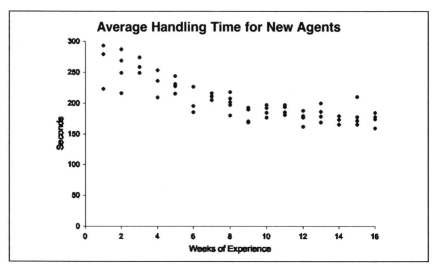

Example applications:

- Average handling time vs. experience level
- Average handling time vs. revenue generated
- Service level vs. error rate
- Experience level vs. quality scores

See System of Causes.

Schedule. A plan that specifies when employees will be on duty, and which may indicate specific activities that they are to handle at specific times. A schedule includes the days worked, start times and stop times, breaks, paid and unpaid status, etc. See Schedule Alternatives.

Schedule Alternatives. Many scheduling alternatives exist that can help the call center efficiently meet staffing requirements that fluctuate throughout the day, week, month and year. Not all are practical in each case. This aspect of planning involves "putting the cards on the table" – identifying the scheduling approaches that are feasible in your environment. Examples include:

- Utilize conventional shifts. Many call centers have a core group of agents that work traditional five-day-a-week shifts during "normal hours" (e.g., 9:00 a.m. to 5:00 p.m.).
- Stagger shifts. For example, one shift begins at 7:00 a.m., the next at 7:30 a.m., the next at 8:00 a.m., until the center is fully staffed for the busy mid-morning traffic. This is a common and effective approach.

- Adjust breaks, lunch, meeting and training schedules. Even slight changes to when these activities are scheduled can mean that a few more people are handling contacts at just the right times. And that can make a big difference. (See Queue Dynamics, and notice the impact of just one person on service level when it is low.)

- Forecast and plan for regular collateral work. Collateral work provides flexibility, if it is planned for and managed well. The objective is to have "all hands on deck" when the call load is high, and assign the flexible tasks to slower periods.

- Schedule part-timers. Some call centers are prevented from using part-time help by union agreements or logistics (e.g., complex call center services requiring extensive training). But when available and practical, this is a popular and common strategy.

- Establish "internal" part-timers. This approach is sometimes called the "reinforcement method." When phone answering duties are combined with other types of tasks, such as correspondence, outbound calling or data-entry, the agents assigned to these collateral duties can act as reinforcements when the calling load gets heavy. This is like begin able to bring in part-timers on an hourly, half-hourly or even five-minute basis.

- Create a "swat team." This takes the reinforcement method one step further, and solicits help from other departments ("reservists") when necessary. This approach is not common, but it is gaining acceptance. Are your contacts important enough to warrant at least some additional help from people elsewhere in the organization? Setup is not trivial. Plan on tackling training, scheduling, pay and cultural issues.

- Offer concentrated shifts. "Four-by-10" shifts are particularly popular with many agents (four days on for 10 hours each, with three days off). But an important consideration is whether they can handle the longer hours without losing effectiveness.

- Offer overtime. No additional training is required and many agents will volunteer for the extra work. But overtime can be expensive as an ongoing strategy. Further, as with concentrated shifts, an important consideration is whether agents can remain effective in extended hours.

- Give agents the option to go home without pay. This is a popular strategy on slower days, and there are usually enough agents willing to take you up on it. It's something referred to as LWOP (leave without pay, pronounced "el-wop").

- Offer split shifts. Split shifts, where agents work a partial shift, take part of the day off, then return later to finish their shift, are not common. But it works in some cases (e.g., with college students who need to take classes in the afternoon but are available in the mornings and evenings).

- Arrange for some agents to be "on call." Although this strategy is impractical for many and is not common, it can work in situations where events cannot be precisely predicted (e.g., catalog companies during the initial days of a new promotion). Typically, agents must either live near the call center or be equipped to telecommute.

- Set up a telecommuting program. This is not a scheduling alternative, per se, but it can provide an environment in which unpopular shifts can be more palatable and enable agents to begin handling the workload on short notice.

- Use hiring to your advantage. An important criteria when hiring new agents should be the hours they can (or can't) work.

- Send calls to a service bureau. Today, service bureaus of all types and capabilities are available. Some can handle calls of virtually any type or degree of complexity.

- Collaborate with similar organizations. In some cases, organizations with different busy seasons have collaborated to share staff.

- Sacrifice service level for a planned period of time. It may be unrealistic for some customer service centers to meet service level objectives during the initial weeks of a new product introduction, or during the busiest season. Consequently, some plan to "sacrifice" service level for three to six weeks and rely on customers to understand. This must be carefully planned and, to be acceptable to callers, it must fall within the realm of their expectations.

In short, there are many scheduling alternatives available, even in relatively restrictive environments. Related terms: Adherence to Schedule, Collateral Duties, Concentrated Shift, Internal Part-Timers, Leave Without Pay (LWOP), Outsourcing, Overtime, Real-Time Adherence Software, Schedule, Schedule Exception, Schedule Horizon, Schedule Preference, Staggered Shifts, Swat Team, Telecommuting.

Schedule Compliance. See Adherence to Schedule.

Schedule Exception. An activity not planned in an employee's schedule, which becomes an "exception" to the plan. Related terms: Adherence to Schedule, Schedule, Schedule Alternatives.

Schedule Horizon. How far in advance schedules are determined. If schedules are determined further out, say for three months or more, they will be somewhat less efficient since they will be locked in place, even if call load deviates from the forecast. However, longer schedule horizons will be more agreeable to your staff, who prefer to know their work schedules well in advance. On the other hand, if you use a shorter horizon, the scheduling process will be less popular with some agents, but schedules will likely be more accurate. Establishing the best scheduling horizon for your center is a balancing act. Related terms: Schedule, Schedule Alternatives, Schedule Preference.

Schedule Preference. A description of the times and days that an employee prefers to work. This can be entered into the scheduling process to ensure that schedules match preferences as closely as possible. Related terms: Schedule, Schedule Alternatives, Schedule Horizon.

Schedule Trade. When agents are allowed to trade schedules. Although popular with agents, the parameters of these arrangements must be carefully defined by management to ensure that the call center has the right people with the right skill sets in the right places at the right times. Related terms: Schedule, Schedule Alternatives, Schedule Preference.

Scheduled Callback. A specified time that the call center will call a customer.

Scheduled Response Time. See Response Time.

Scheduled Staff vs. Actual. A performance measure that is a comparison of the number of agents scheduled vs. the number actually in the center, involved in the activities specified by the schedule. This measure is independent of whether or not you actually have the staff necessary to achieve a targeted service level and/or response time. It is simply a comparison of how closely reality aligned with the schedules you established. The purpose of the objective is to understand and improve staff adherence and schedules. Related term: Adherence to Schedule.

Scope. See Project Management.

Screen Monitoring. A system capability that enables a supervisor or manager to remotely monitor the activity on agents' computer terminals. See Monitoring.

Screen Pop. A CTI application that delivers an incoming call to an agent, along with the data screen pertaining to that call or caller. Callers' records are retrieved based on ANI or digits entered into the VRU. Also called coordinated voice/data delivery. See Computer Telephony Integration.

Screen Refresh. The rate at which real-time information is updated on a display (e.g., every five to 15 seconds). Screen refresh does not correlate with the timeframe used for real-time calculations.

Screening Tools. Tools that enable employers to determine whether a job candidate is fit for the position. There are many variations of screening tools, from simple to involved, low-tech to high-tech. Examples include application forms, resumes and cover letters, tests (e.g., performance, psychological or job-match tests), work samples, recommendations from others and reference checks. See Recruiting.

Script. The words, logic or flow to be followed when handling a contact. Scripts are designed to assist agents in handling contacts. Strict definitions of scripts refer to detail right down to the words that agents are to use in conversations. But scripts also refer to call logic and call flows where word choice is up to the agent but call flow is suggested by the script.

Scripting. Sometimes referred to as "dialog manager." An application that provides scripts to agents to aid in call handling (e.g., product description, promotional offer, wrap-up information). Scripts can generally be controlled and modified to accommodate various situations and individuals (e.g., different levels of experience, full scripts vs. reminder lists, generic or customized). (Vanguard)

Seated Agents. See Base Staff.

Self-Service System. A system that enables customers to access the information or services they need without interacting with an agent. Web capabilities that enable online sales or services and IVR applications that provide automated flight information or access to financial accounts are common examples of self-service systems.

Call centers play an important role in ensuring the success of these systems. For example, call centers have the opportunity to:

- Equip agents to educate customers on self-service options.
- Collect and analyze data about calls currently handled in the call center. This data can identify self-service features that callers will want to use.
- Observe agents at work. Self-service systems can often be modeled after effective agent practices.
- Analyze call monitoring data and quality results (e.g., are agents referring callers to automated options when feasible?).

- Integrate self-service and call center systems and developments. The call center should be involved with self-service systems, from development through implementation and maintenance phases.
- Capture caller feedback about self-service systems. This information is essential to identifying problem issues and improving system design.
- Enable customers to easily reach agents as needed.

Self-service systems must be an integrated part of a customer access strategy with their purpose clearly defined. By keeping the focus on cultivating better ways to serve customers, self-service systems can become an important part of building valuable services and minimizing costs.

Server. A computer that shares its resources with other computers on a network. For example, file servers share disk storage with other computers. Database servers respond to requests from other computers on the network (clients) with specific data records. Application servers respond to requests from clients for processing or presentation of data. Related term: Desktop Technologies. (Vanguard)

Service Bureau. A service bureau, sometimes referred to as an outsourcer, is a company hired to handle some or all of the organization's contacts. Service bureaus of all types and capabilities are available. See Outsourcing.

Service Level. Also called telephone service factor (TSF). Service level is defined specifically as: "X percent of contacts answered in Y seconds"; e.g., 90 percent answered in 20 seconds. Contacts that must be handled when they arrive require a service level objective, and those that can be handled at a later time require a response time objective. (See Response Time.)

The principle of service level, sometimes generally referred to as "accessibility," is at the heart of effective call center management. Without service level objectives, answers to many important questions would be left to chance. For example:

- How accessible is the call center?
- How many staff do you need?
- How do you compare to the competition?
- Are you prepared to handle the response to marketing campaigns?
- How busy are your agents going to be?
- What are your costs going to be?

While there is no industry standard service level, the following table illustrates typical service level objectives:

General Comparisons*	Service Levels (X percent/Y seconds)
Emergency Services (e.g., 911 call centers)	100/0
SL objectives that are comparatively "high"	90/20, 85/15
SL objectives that are comparatively "moderate"	80/20, 90/60
SL objectives that are comparatively "modest"	90/120, 80/300

* from industry surveys

Service level ties the resources you need to the results you want to achieve. It measures how well you are getting the transactions "in the door" and to agents so that you can get on with the business at hand, and it's a stable, concrete target for planning and budgeting.

When establishing and assessing either service level or response time objectives, remember that it's not just how high your overall stated objectives are, but how consistently you hit them throughout the day. Related Terms: Response Time, Service Level Agreement, Service Level Calculations.

Service Level Agreement (SLA). An agreement, usually between a client organization and an outsourcer (although they increasingly exist between departments within an organization), that defines performance objectives and expectations. Common components of a service level agreement include:

- Service level and response time objectives
- Hours of operation
- Forecasted workload
- Abandoned call objectives
- First-call resolution
- Services provided
- Products supported
- Quality procedures and standards
- Reporting requirements, methodology and timelines
- Disaster recovery expectations and procedures
- Escalation procedures.

The establishment of SLAs helps client organizations overcome concerns about the quality of work that will be handled by the outsourcer or other department. In addition, written SLAs provide objectives and timeframes by which to measure performance, eliminate confusion regarding expectations (e.g., clearly outline forecasted workloads, establish first-call resolution goals), put both organizations on the "same page" regarding objectives, and establish a formal process for communicating expectations. See Outsourcer.

Service Level Calculations. There are a number of alternative methods your call center technology may use to calculate service level. With some systems, you can specify the calculation you prefer. Here are the most common formulas:

1. (Calls answered in Y seconds + calls abandoned in Y seconds) ÷ (total calls answered + total calls abandoned). For most situations, this is a preferred approach because the calculation includes all of the traffic received by the automatic call distributor (ACD). This calculation provides a complete picture of what is happening since it takes all calls into consideration.

2. Calls answered in Y seconds ÷ total calls answered. This alternative only considers answered calls, and therefore is not a good reflection of all activity. Abandonment is entirely ignored.

3. Calls answered in Y seconds ÷ (total calls answered + total calls abandoned). This alternative tends to be the least popular among call center managers because all calls that abandon negatively affect service level, even those that abandon before the objective. This measure is appropriate in situations where calls enter a queue after they hear a delay announcement.

4. Calls answered in Y seconds ÷ (total calls answered + calls abandoned after Y seconds). With this calculation, abandoned calls only impact service level negatively if they happen after the Y seconds specified. Calls that abandon before the objective do not affect service level. Consequently, this is a way to avoid getting "penalized" by callers who abandon quickly without ignoring abandoned calls altogether. This is an acceptable approach.

Related terms: Queue Dynamics, Service Level.

Service Observing. See Monitoring.

Service-Oriented Organizational Design. See Organizational Design.

Service Quality. See Call Quality.

Session Initiation Protocol (SIP). An IETF pending standard for

VoIP, utilizing Internet-based development tools. SIP holds the promise of being less complex than H.323. Related term: H.323. (Vanguard)

Shrink Factor. See Rostered Staff Factor.

Shrinkage. See Rostered Staff Factor.

Side-by-Side Monitoring. See Monitoring.

Signaling System 7 (SS7). A method of signaling within the voice network that uses a separate packet-switched data network (common channel signaling) to communicate information about calls. In a multisite virtual call center environment that is CTI-enabled and conducting pre-arrival routing, SS7 can be used to pass information in order to decide which site is "best" to route the call. (Vanguard)

Silent Monitoring. See Monitoring.

Simple Mail Transfer Protocol (SMTP). A standard for sending email used by most email systems. Used for transmission of email over the Internet. (Vanguard)

Simplified Message Desk Interface (SMDI). An industry standard method of integrating voicemail systems with digital PBXs. The standard is defined by Bellcore for use with Centrex style technologies, and is a common method of integrating the two systems. It uses a data communication link to permit transfer of information over an RS-232 link to the voice-processing module. (Vangaurd)

Simplified Network Management Protocol (SNMP). A protocol from the TCP/IP suite that enables network devices to be remotely monitored and managed by a network management system. Related term: Network Management System. (Vanguard)

Simulation Tools. See Computer Simulation.

Site Selection. The process of choosing a call center location that best meets the needs of the organization. Site selection considerations include:

- Labor issues
- Telecommunications considerations
- Real estate design and cost issues
- Government incentives, taxation and legislation

Because labor often constitutes 60 percent or more of call center oper-

ating costs, it is the most important site selection consideration. Labor
issues include:

* Size of the labor pool
* Population inflow or outflow
* Demographics
* Skill requirements
* Quality of life and community

Related term: Economic Development Agency.

Six Sigma. Originally developed by Motorola, Six Sigma is a highly disciplined process that focuses on developing and delivering near-perfect
products and services. Sigma is a statistical term that measures process
variation. The intent behind Six Sigma is to measure and isolate variation
and defects in processes and products in order to get as close to "zero
defects" as possible. Six Sigma has become widespread, and Six Sigma
training programs and support materials are available throughout the
world from many sources. See System of Causes.

Skill Group. See Agent Group.

Skill Path. Skill paths focus on the development of specific skills rather
than the progression of positions through the center and/or organization.
Skill paths can move laterally (e.g., a printer technical support agent can
be cross-trained to handle technical support on fax machines, as well) or
upward (e.g., an agent can acquire leadership and coaching skills to add
peer coaching responsibilities to his or her current position).

Because the historical corporate-ladder approach to staff development
can be limited for call centers (due to the finite amount of supervisory
and management positions available), a more effective staff development
approach may be the skill path model. Skill paths seek to prepare agents
for the future of the organization's business by taking into consideration
individual staff needs and organizational goals. Individuals often receive
more compensation as they achieve new skill levels within their position.
It is easier to get executive-level support and funding for skill paths if they
are aligned with overall business needs.

The terms career path and skill path are often used interchangeably
since the differentiation is often only one of emphasis: career paths focus
on progressing to new positions while skill paths are associated with
acquiring new skills and responsibilities without necessarily changing job
titles. See Career Path.

Skills-Based Routing (SBR). Skills-based routing matches a caller's specific needs with an agent who has the skills to handle that call on a real-time basis. SBR requires that the ACD be programmed with two "maps"; one map specifies the types of calls to be handled (e.g., gold-level, Spanish-speaking) and the other identifies the skills available by agent (e.g., Maria is capable of handling platinum, gold and silver calls, and she speaks English and Spanish).

The basic requirements to get started with skills-based routing include:

- Identify what differentiates caller needs and desires. This comes from the customer access strategy.
- Identify and define the skills required for each call type.
- Identify and define individual agent skills.
- Prioritize agent skills, based on individual competency levels.
- Devise and program into the ACD an appropriate routing plan.

In general, skills-based routing works best in environments that have small groups where multiple skills are required. It can also help to quickly integrate new agents into call handling, by sending only simple calls to them. It also has the potential to improve efficiency by matching callers with "just the right agent."

In this environment, Erlang C's assumption of traditional ACD groups no longer fits, but computer simulation can help fill the gap. Be prepared to run enough simulations to learn what's workable in your environment. You also need to develop contingency plans – when the call load of a specific call type is greater than expected or when you don't have the specialized staff for which you planned (e.g., because of sickness).

Skills-based routing has some disadvantages. Getting people in the right place at the right times can be difficult, and small specialized groups are tough to manage. And they can eliminate the efficiencies of pooling, common to conventional ACD groups. Further, routing and resource planning becomes more complex.

Skills-based routing is a powerful capability. But it must be managed well – you will need a good forecast and solid staff calculations. Related terms: Agent Group, Computer Simulation, Customer Access Strategy, Erlang C, Pooling Principle.

Small Office Home Office (SOHO). As the term implies, SOHO is a general reference to small offices or offices located in homes; may also refer to individuals who work out of small or home offices.

Smooth Call Arrival. Calls that arrive evenly across a period of time. Virtually non-existent in incoming call center environments. See Traffic Arrival.

Snapshot Survey. One-shot survey that is intended to measure objectives at a single point in time. See Customer Survey.

Soft-Dollar Savings. See Hard-Dollar Savings.

Softphone. The ability to access telephony functions through a PC desktop computer interface instead of a telephone. For a call center agent, softphone can include login/logout to both the voice and data systems via a single action on the PC, point-and-click changing of work states (available, unavailable/not ready), visibility into availability and statistics, outbound calling, and entry of transaction codes via the PC. Softphone is a CTI-enabled function. (Vanguard)

Span of Control. The number of individuals a manager supervises. A large span of control means that the manager supervises many people. A small span of control means the manager supervisors fewer people. Span of control decreases as the complexity and variability of the conditions in the environment increase.

Effective ratios are dependent on the tasks, standards and responsibilities of both agents and supervisors. Many call centers have between 10 and 20 staff per supervisor, with 12 to 15 being the most common range. However, there are notable differences by industry. For example, help desks and insurance companies tend to be on the low end of that spectrum (have smaller spans of control), while catalog companies and telecommunications services providers tend to be on the high end.

In terms of supervisor-to-management spans of control, ratios of between 5:1 and 12:1 are typical. Given the higher level and more complex interactions that must take place between managers and supervisors, spans of control are smaller than those for agents/supervisors. That underscores a principle generally true in most organizations: the higher up in the organization, the smaller the spans of control. Related terms: Agent Group, Organizational Design.

Speaker Verification. A method of verifying the identity of a caller by comparing his voice to a previously stored voiceprint. Also referred to as voice authentication. See Speech Recognition. (Vanguard)

Special Causes. Variation in a process caused by special or unusual circumstances. Related terms: Common Causes, Control Chart.

Specialized Agent Group. See Agent Group.

Speech Recognition. Speech recognition enables IVR systems to interact with databases using spoken language, rather than the telephone keypad. A well-designed speech recognition application will attract customers who would not otherwise successfully complete self-service transactions.

There are two key types of speech recognition used in call centers today:

- Directed dialogue or structured language: This type of prompting coaches the caller through the selections. For example, a bank application might say: "What would you like to do? You can say 'get balance,' 'transfer funds' or 'explore specific transactions.'"

- Natural language: This type uses a more open-ended prompt, recognizing what the caller says without as much coaching. The caller can speak naturally (e.g., responding to a prompt about what they would like to do with "Um, I'd like to transfer funds from my checking account to my savings account"). Speech applications are speaker independent, recognizing a variety of accents and colloquialisms.

Vocabularies of speech-based systems are in the tens of thousands of words enabling applications that are otherwise too complex for touchtone, such as stock and fund quotes and travel status. See Interactive Voice Response.

Split. See Agent Group.

Split Shifts. Shifts in which agents work a partial shift, take part of the day off, then return later to finish their shift. This scheduling alternative is not common, but works well in some situations. For example, college students may prefer to work in the mornings and evenings, leaving afternoons free for classes. Related terms: Schedule, Schedule Alternatives.

Staff Sharing. A staff-sharing relationship is when two or more organizations (or different units of an organization) share a common pool of employees, typically to meet seasonal demands. For example, an organization with a heavy summer workload may partner with an organization that is busiest in winter months to share staff. Staff-sharing relationships are, as of yet, uncommon in the call center industry. But they have been proven successful, and will likely become more common in the future. Related terms: Schedule, Schedule Alternatives.

Staff-to-Supervisor Ratio. See Span of Control.

Staggered Shifts. Shifts that begin and end at different times. For example, one shift begins at 7 a.m., the next at 7:30 a.m., the next at 8 a.m., until the center is fully staffed for the busy midmorning traffic. Related terms: Schedule, Schedule Alternatives.

Stakeholders. Individuals or organizations with a share or interest in the organization, including employees, customers, investors, suppliers and vendors, resellers and distributors, and lawmakers.

Standalone ACD. See Automatic Call Distributor (ACD).

Standard. A quantifiable minimum level of performance; performance below or outside the standard is not acceptable.

Standard Generalized Markup Language (SGML). Web pages are usually encoded with tags called Hypertext Markup Language (HTML); SGML is the tag-set building rules (the parent language) for HTML and other descriptive tag-sets. The official definition of SGML is in the international standard ISO 8879:1986.

Statement of Retained Earnings. The statement of retained earnings is typically presented at the bottom of the P&L, in the equity section of the balance sheet or as a separate sheet in the annual report. According to *Barron's*, "Retained earnings for a firm equals total earnings to date less total dividends to date, adjusted by other transactions in some cases." Related terms: Balance Sheet, Income Statement, Cash-Flow Statement.

Station Message Detail Recording (SMDR). See Call Detail Recording.

Strategic Business Plan. A strategic business plan usually refers to the general plan that consolidates and summarizes the various plans and strategies required to meet strategic objectives. The strategic business plan usually looks several years into the future and summarizes plans and strategies related to recruiting and hiring, training, processes, technologies, communication, budgets and investments, and so on. It includes the process of identifying opportunities and threats that drive decision-making.

Key to developing a strategic business plan is effective communication, a supportive culture and the commitment of senior management. Since it has a relatively long-term strategic focus, specific tactical challenges are less influential. A strategic business plan is generally more dynamic – changes more frequently – than an operational model. Related terms: Annual Operating Plan, Customer Access Strategy, Operational Model, Organizational Design, Strategy.

Strategic Staffing Plan. A forecast of future staffing requirements – which includes quantity and qualifications – generally over a one- to three-year timeframe. The plan focuses on three major issues:

1. The number of staff required
2. Required staff qualifications and associated development plans
3. Feasible workforce mix and scheduling alternatives

Related terms: Customer Access Strategy, Full-Time Equivalent, Schedule Alternatives.

Strategy. The overall approach for accomplishing the organization's mission. Strategy must be developed on two general levels: The organization's overarching strategy and business unit strategies, which must work together to support the organization's overall strategy, vision and mission.

Without effective strategy, even the most compelling visions will go nowhere. Strategy provides the overall framework for how the organization will turn the vision into reality. It creates tangible advantages that result in a whole greater than the sum of its parts. It provides the mechanism through which daily activities and priorities are established.

Common organizationwide strategies include:

- Cost Leadership: With this strategy, the intent is to achieve a cost leadership position through policies, practices, procedures and actions that enable the organization to be the low-cost provider. Management is focused on cost control in areas such as scale, overhead control, avoidance of marginal customer accounts, etc. The intent is that low-cost production will result in an above average return on the organization's investments.

- Differentiation: This strategy involves differentiating the organization by creating product and service offerings that are perceived by the market as unique. Differentiation can take the form of design or brand image, technology, features, customer service and quality. Effective differentiation can create brand loyalty and provide a safety net against price sensitivity. Because it increases margins, it can reduce the need to be a low-cost provider.

- Focus: This strategy involves targeting defined customer groups, product lines or geographic markets in order to serve those segments better than competitors. Functional policies are developed with this intent in mind. A combination of organizational requirements focused at strategic markets or customer segments is required.

- Defender: This strategy is often pursued by organizations with a significant market share and with a stable market, customer base and line of products and services. Defenders do not generally seek new markets, but instead are focused on protecting the market share they have (e.g., developing brand loyalty). There is usually much emphasis placed on management control, policies, effective processes and procedures, and detailed planning.

- Prospector: This strategy is pursued by organizations that move aggressively in the market. They are generally highly competitive, innovative and focused on speed to market. They generally operate in markets that are rapidly changing.

A wide variety of analysts and scholars have presented alternative frameworks. For example, Michael Treacy and Fred Wiersema, in *The Discipline of Market Leaders*, cite only three corporate operating models: operational excellence, product leadership and customer intimacy. In *Strategy Safari*, Bruce Ahlstrand, Joseph Lampel and Henry Mintzberg group strategy formation into 10 overall schools of thought, ranging from a visionary process to a process of transformation – each with different frameworks and outcomes. In the call center environment, strategy is embodied in what is often termed a customer access strategy. Related terms: Customer Access Strategy, Organizational Design.

Structured Interview. An interview based on the job description for the position. Consistent questions are developed based on job responsibilities and competencies, and standard criteria are used for ranking or rating candidates. See Unstructured Interview.

Structured Language. See Directed Dialog.

Structured Query Language (SQL). A language developed by IBM for requesting data from relational databases. (Vanguard)

Succession Planning. The identification and preparation of high-potential individuals for senior-level positions.

Suggestive Selling. See Cross-Sell and Upsell.

Super Agent. See Universal Agent.

Supervisor. The person who has frontline responsibility for a group of agents. Generally, supervisors are equipped with special telephones and computer terminals that enable them to monitor agent activities.

Several years ago, many call center managers along with most industry pundits were predicting that supervisors would become less important in call centers, and that their numbers would begin to decline. The conventional rationale was that because agents and teams were becoming more empowered, the need for a layer between management and the front line would decline. However, it has become clear that the role of supervisor is as important and prevalent as ever. By most indications, call centers today have proportionally more supervisors than at any other time in call center history.

So why were the predictions largely wrong? Most call center managers point to growing complexity and variety in the workload, along with greater emphasis on handling difficult calls without further transactions or escalation. But there are also other factors at work.

For example, monitoring and coaching remain the two most time-consuming activities for most supervisors. But they are increasingly involved in leveraging the knowledge gained from these efforts into more lasting and significant process improvements. They are spending less time making improvements one agent at a time – the "personal trainer" approach – and more time working with their peers in other areas to improve training, information, communication and procedures throughout the call center.

They are also more involved in call center planning and management. When supervisors are involved in forecasting, scheduling and other planning processes, they not only contribute their perspective, they also gain a better understanding of the factors that contribute to service level and quality. As a result, they more effectively supervise their teams.

Related terms: Job Role, Monitoring, Span of Control.

Supervisor Monitor. Computer monitors that enable supervisors to monitor the call handling statistics of their supervisory groups or teams.

Suspect Performance Driver. A performance driver that has been attributed to results, but with an unproven linkage. Most people will have their own mental lists of suspected performance drivers. See Performance Driver.

Swat Team. The term some companies use for a team of non call center employees that can act as "reservists" to quickly be assigned to call handling duties if the call load soars. Related terms: Schedule, Schedule Alternatives.

Switch. A device that connects other devices for communication. The term can refer to a data switch or a voice switch. (Vanguard)

Switchboard. The attendant position of a telephone system, usually where calls coming into a main number of a company are answered and distributed by the switchboard operator.

System of Causes. A call center is a process or system of causes. Taking a larger view, the call center is part of a larger process, the organization. In a lesser view, each agent group in a call center is a system of causes unto itself, as are individual agents in a group. The central focus of the process can be any KPI or virtually any other measure or objective.

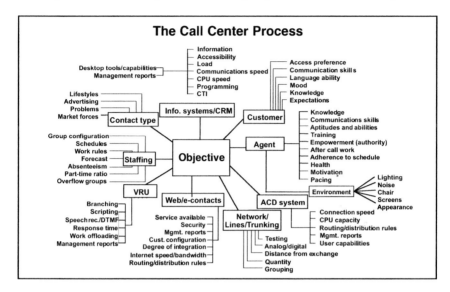

The Call Center Process

Note that just about everything is interrelated, so the causes of performance problems are often difficult to isolate and measure. Tracking high-level measurements won't inherently improve them. To make improvements, you have to work on the factors that cause these outputs to be what they are. In other words, you have to work at a deeper level, the root causes. Related terms: Root Cause, Six Sigma.

Systems Integrator. A consulting firm or systems supplier that coordinates the installation and setup of complex systems. For example, call center applications may need to be integrated with legacy systems, requiring complex programming and project management.

T1 Circuit. A high-speed digital circuit used for voice, data or video with a bandwidth of 1.544 megabits per second. T1 circuits offer the equivalent of 24 analog voice lines. The European equivalent is known as E1 and it offers the equivalent of 31 analog voice lines. (Vanguard)

Talk Time. Everything from "hello" to "goodbye." In other words, it's the time callers are connected with agents. Anything that happens during talk time, such as placing customers on hold to confer with supervisors, should be included in this measurement. Also called direct call processing. Related terms: After-Call Work, Call Load.

Team. A group of individuals with complementary skills who are committed to a common purpose and performance goals to which they hold themselves mutually accountable. The purpose of creating a team is to bring together people whose work is related and interdependent. The team enables them to work in a more collaborative manner to achieve individual, call center and organizational objectives.

The subject of teams in call centers is not a firmly defined issue. Depending on the size of the center, the types of contacts that are handled and the organizational culture, one agent team may be a subset of an agent queue group or may include several agent queue groups. Supervisors may be responsible for several agent teams or there may be several supervisors responsible for different members of one team. The scenario that is most effective in your environment can only be determined through careful consideration of the culture, workload and objectives of your center.

There are several types of teams, which can be categorized by function, structure and skill:

- A functional team is based on the purpose for forming the team. For example, a task force could be a functional team formed to study a particular situation such as inaccurate forecasts or innovation opportunities.

- Team types may also be categorized according to their structure. The crossfunctional team is an example of a team structure. In this case, team members are comprised of individuals from several organizational functions. This team structure brings different perspectives and expertise to bear on an organizational problem or opportunity.

- In a skill-oriented team, the commonality of skill sets form the basis for the team. For example, call centers may organize coaches into quality teams to facilitate consistency and shared team focus on quality objectives.

These types of teams are not mutually exclusive. For example, you could easily have a crossfunctional task force to address a problem or opportunity.

Team-Oriented Organizational Design. See Organizational Design.

Technology Adoption Lifecycle. Generally attributed to consultant Geoffrey Moore, the model forms a bell curve with five divisions that describe psychographic buying habits. The technology adoption lifecycle offers a practical model for call center managers to apply when evaluating new technology.

The five divisions of the model are:

- Innovators: Sometimes referred to as "technology enthusiasts," these folks buy into new technology early and often. They love trying new things, and typically will do what they can to help the supplier bring the product to the marketplace.

- Early Adopters: Also called "visionaries," they are quick to understand and appreciate the benefits of new technologies, and are willing to take some risks to realize potential order-of-magnitude gains that can come from being among the first to embrace new capabilities.

- Early Majority: Also referred to as "pragmatists," members of this large group are driven by a strong sense of practicality. They share some of the characteristics of early adopters, but they prefer to wait until the market "shakes out" and the technology is more proven. Moore suggests that once a technology crosses the "chasm" between early adopters and early majority, it will rapidly proliferate, bringing a flood of business to suppliers and competitive pressures to end-users to get on board.

- Late Majority: These "conservatives" want solutions that work, with little risk and few implementation hassles. Like the early majority, they have a strong sense of practicality, but would rather wait until turnkey solutions with well-defined ROIs are available.

- Laggards: Members of this group resist new technology and distrust conventional competitive and productivity-improvement arguments. These "skeptics" are generally viewed by vendors as not worth the effort. Related terms: Customer Access Strategy, Risk.

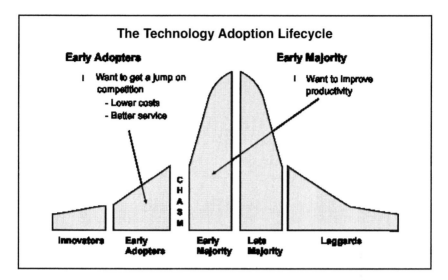

The Technology Adoption Lifecycle

Technology-Based Training (TBT). Training that uses technology to deliver instruction, typically outside of the formal classroom environment. TBT can include the use of computers or other technologies such as video or audiotape. Computer-based training is a type of TBT. Related terms: Computer-Based Training, Training, Training Strategy.

Telco. An abbreviation for telephone company.

Telecommuting. Using telecommunications to work from home or other locations instead of at the organization's premises. Related terms: Remote Agent, Scheduling Alternatives.

Telemarketing. Generally refers to outbound calls for the purpose of selling products or services, or placing informational calls to customers, prospective customers or constituents.

Telephone Sales or Service Representative (TSR). See Agent.

Telephone Service Factor (TSF). See Service Level.

Telephony Application Programming Interface (TAPI). An API developed by Microsoft and Intel to enable computer-telephony functions on Windows-based systems. It is one of the de facto standards by virtue of Microsoft's large installed base. (Vanguard)

Telephony Services Application Programming Interface (TSAPI). A CTI API developed by Novell and AT&T/Lucent/Avaya. (Vanguard)

Temporary Employee. An employee hired for short-term projects or seasonal workloads. Temporary employees, often called "temps," are typically a good fit for assignments that last six to nine months or less. These positions can be filled either through a company's internal hiring process or, more commonly, through the use of an external temporary agency. Temporaries often thrive in organizations with relatively short (e.g., two weeks or less) training times, flexible scheduling policies and quick calls that are relatively simple to handle. In more complex environments requiring longer training periods, temporary employees often are not the best fit. Temporary employees may become a source for employee recruitment. See Temporary-to-Permanent Placement.

Temporary-to-Permanent Placement. With this arrangement, job candidates are initially hired as an employee of the staffing agency and contracted on a temporary basis to the organization. This arrangement dictates that within a certain period of time the employee will be hired by the organization permanently, provided his or her performance meets expectations. The organization may participate in the interviewing and hiring decision or they may rely on the staffing agency to handle the hiring process from start to finish. See Temporary Employee.

Text-Chat Application. Allows customers visiting the corporate Web site to have real-time, text-based conversations with live agents. Text-chat applications also can provide agents with appropriate text templates to insert in their responses. They can enable agents to co-browse Web pages with customers and "push" specific pages to the customer. Agents can also be enabled to move the customer's cursor and help fill in complex forms and applications.

Text-to-Speech (TTS). Enables a voice processing system to speak the words in a text field using synthesized – not recorded – speech. Sometimes used for large, dynamic database applications where it is impractical to record all speech phrases, such as addresses or product names. Also used to "read" email or other text-based information over the telephone. (Vanguard)

Thick Client. A workstation in a client/server environment that performs much or most of the application processing. It requires programs and data to be installed on it and a significant part of the application processing takes place on the workstation. The client is "thick" in that it has much of the smarts of the overall application running on it. Related terms: Client, Thin Client. (Vanguard)

Thin Client. A workstation in a client/server environment that performs little or no application processing. Often used to describe browser-based desktops. The client is "thin" in that the applications reside on and are run within the server rather than the client. Related terms: Client, Thick Client. (Vanguard)

Three-Tier Architecture. An information system architecture where processing functionality is split into three discrete functions: 1) presentation (desktop PC), 2) application (business rules), and 3) data (database system). By keeping the functionality cleanly separated, three-tier architectures are scalable and flexible. (Vanguard)

Threshold. The point at which an action, change or process takes place.

Tie Line. A private circuit that connects two ACDs or PBXs across a wide area.

Tiered Scheduling. An approach to allocating resources that defines a range of staffing requirements for a given time interval and places individuals in separate groups (tiers) within that range. For example, tier 1 may be scheduled for phone duty regardless of queuing conditions, but tier 3 won't sign on unless there are 15 or more calls in queue. Related terms: Schedule, Schedule Alternatives.

Time-of-Day Effectiveness. An outbound term, refers to the periods of the day when the most contacts are made. This is the most important driver of optimum staffing in an outbound environment.

Time-Series Forecasting. See Forecasting Methodologies.

Title VII of the U.S. Civil Rights Act of 1964. Prohibits discrimination based on race, color, gender, religion or national origin. Later laws expanded the interpretation of the Act to include discrimination based on age, disability, veteran status and other factors.

Toll-Free Service. Enables callers to reach a call center out of the local calling area without incurring charges. 800/888/877/866 et al. is toll-free. In some countries, there are also other variations of toll-free service. For example, with 0345 or 0645 services in the United Kingdom, callers are charged local rates and the call center pays for the long-distance charges.

Touchtone. A trademark of AT&T. See Dual-Tone Multifrequency.

Traffic Arrival. To correctly manage a call center that handles inbound contacts, you need to know whether traffic arrival will be random, smooth or peaked. Telecommunications traffic engineers have assigned statistical "variance-to-mean" ratios to designate each type of traffic, but, essentially, the patterns look like this:

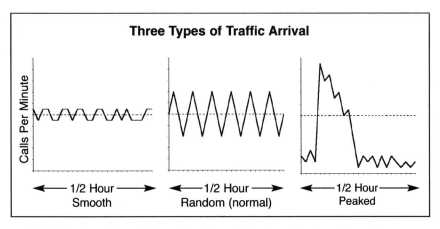

Three Types of Traffic Arrival

Following is a description of each, and the implications for call centers:

- Random (Normal) Call Arrival: Calls arrive randomly most of the time in the vast majority of inbound call centers. Exactly when calls arrive from moment to moment is the result of decisions made by callers who are motivated by a myriad of individual needs and conditions. Put another way, calls "bunch up." Staffing must be calculated by using either a queuing formula that takes random call arrival into account (generally Erlang C) or a computer simulation program that accurately models this phenomenon. And because staffing impacts the load the network and systems must carry, miscalculated staff inherently leads to miscalculated system and network resources. Also, performance objectives and standards must take random call arrival into account. For example, a standard of "N widgets per day" may make sense in a traditional assembly-line setting, but it doesn't work in an environment where the workload arrives randomly.

- Smooth Traffic: Smooth traffic is virtually nonexistent in incoming call centers, but can apply in outbound environments. For example, a group of people may be assigned to make outbound calls, one after another, for the duration of their shift. In that case, the number of circuits required is equal to the number of agents placing the calls.

- Peaked Traffic: Peaked traffic is a surge of calls beyond random variation (e.g., calls prompted by television or radio ads). Many of us use the term "peak" in a general sense when referring to call traffic (e.g., What's your peak time of year? Peak day of the week? Peak time of day?) But the term "peaked traffic" specifically refers to a surge of traffic beyond random variation. It is a spike within a short period of time. The implications of peaked traffic include: staffing must be calculated at a smaller interval than half-hour, such as 10 minutes or even five minutes; for a given service level, peaked traffic requires more staff than random traffic; how concentrated peaked traffic is within a brief period of time will dramatically impact service level.

Related terms: Computer Simulation, Erlang C, Increments, Queue Dynamics, Service Level.

Traffic Control Center. See Network Control Center.

Traffic Engineering. Designing telecommunications and data systems and networks to meet user requirements. Related terms: Computer Simulation, Erlang B, Erlang C, Traffic Arrival.

Training. Learning with job-specific objectives. Training has a short-term focus. Related terms: Learning, Development, Education, Training Strategy, On-the-Job Training.

Training Evaluation. The process of assessing the impact of a training program. When assessing a training program, there are four levels of evaluation:

- Level 1: Reaction. Reaction comes primarily from evaluations filled out by attendees at the conclusion of the training program. In survey format, it usually covers such items as program methodology, group and individual exercises, quality of materials and media, facilitator capabilities, facilities, etc.

- Level 2: Learning evaluation. This is the process of collecting, analyzing and reporting information to assess how much the participants learned and applied in the learning experience.

- Level 3: Application to job. This step assesses the degree to which the knowledge, skills and abilities taught in the classroom are being used on the job. It includes identification of enablers and barriers that facilitate or inhibit successful application.

- Level 4: Evaluating the impact and ROI. This is the process of determining the impact of training on organizational productivity, improved customer satisfaction, and the organization's strategic business plan.

See Training Strategy.

Training Strategy. A call center training strategy determines intermediate to long-term training priorities, objectives and direction. The training strategy should align with the call center's overall objectives and strategies. There are six primary drivers of call center training:

- Business opportunities or problems
- Management planning
- Changes in technology
- Changing customer requirements
- Political/regulatory changes
- Labor issues (e.g., addressing turnover)

Related terms: Adult Learning, Learning Organization, Training Evaluation.

Transaction. See Call.

Transmission Control Protocol/Internet Protocol (TCP/IP). A standard set of protocols that govern the exchange of data between computing systems. TCP/IP was originally designed by the U.S. Department of Defense to link dissimilar computers across many kinds of networks. It has since become a common standard for commercial equipment and applications. TCP/IP specifies how information that travels over the Internet should be divided and reassembled. In call centers, TCP/IP is the underlying protocol of VoIP. It is also widely used in IVR, CTI and CRM systems. (Vanguard)

Trouble Ticket. The report of a customer's problem with a particular device or system, which is tracked through the workflow process. Trouble tickets were originally written on paper, but electronic trouble tickets are now standard in many workflow and help-desk applications.

True Calls Per Agent. Also called normalized calls per agent. It is actual calls (contacts) an individual or group handled divided by occupancy for that period of time.

The idea behind true calls per agent is to convert raw contacts handled into an adjusted measurement that is more fair and meaningful. For example, occupancy, which is not within the control of an individual, can be "neutralized" by dividing contacts handled by percent occupancy.

Using the numbers in the table, 5.6 average calls per agent divided by 65 percent is 8.6 "normalized" calls, as is 6.7 calls divided by 78 percent, 7.7 calls divided by 90 percent and 8.1 calls divided by 94 percent.

Calls in 1/2 Hour	Service Level	Agents Required	Occupancy	Avg. Calls Per Agent	True Calls Per Agent
50	80/20	9	65%	5.6	8.6
100	80/20	15	78%	6.7	8.6
500	80/20	65	90%	7.7	8.6
1000	80/20	124	94%	8.1	8.6

Assumption: Calls last an average 3.5 minutes.

Others go a step further and develop statistical control charts to determine whether the process is in control, what it's producing and which agents, if any, are outside of "statistical control."

Even true calls per agent begins to lose meaning as technologies such as CTI, skills-based routing and Web integration, which enable increasingly sophisticated and varied call-handling routines, proliferate. Thus the growing acceptance and use of adherence and qualitative measurements. Related terms: Adherence to Schedule, Call Quality, Contacts Handled (Calls Per Agent).

Trunk. Also called a line, exchange line or circuit. A telephone circuit linking two switching systems. See Trunk Load.

Trunk Group. A collection of trunks associated with a single peripheral and usually used for a common purpose. Related terms: Trunk, Trunk Group.

Trunk Load. The load that trunks carry. Includes both delay and talk time. The graph illustrates the difference between agent load and trunk load. Related terms: Erlang B, Queue Dynamics, Trunk, Trunk Group.

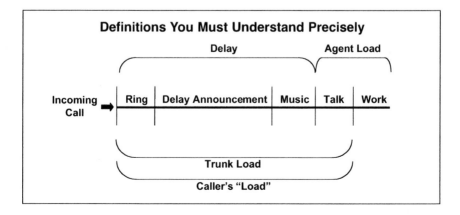

Trunks Idle. The number of trunks in a trunk group that are non-busy.

Trunks in Service. The number of trunks in the trunk group that are functional.

Turnkey. A system that is ready for use right out of the box, or from the moment of installation.

Turnover. When a person leaves the call center. The turnover rate quantifies these employee separations as a percentage of all employees.

Turnover can be categorized as voluntary or involuntary. Voluntary turnover is when the employee decides to leave the organization or position. Involuntary turnover occurs when management makes the decision to end the employment relationship. Turnover can also be categorized as internal turnover, which refers to employees that leave the call center but stay within the organization, and external turnover, which refers to employees that leave the organization entirely.

To measure turnover correctly, call center managers should calculate an annualized turnover rate. An annualized number does not require 12 months worth of data. The annualized figure provides a consistent basis for comparison and trending. The calculation is as follows:

Turnover = (# of agents exiting the job ÷ avg. actual # of agents during the period) x (12 ÷ # mos. in the period)

Input for Turnover Calculation

	# of agents exiting the job during month	Avg. # of agents on staff during month*
January	2	104
February	1	103
March	4	101
April	0	101
May	3	109
June	5	106
July	2	105
August	3	103
Total/Average	20	104

*The average number of agents on staff during the month is often calculated by taking an average of the counts at the end of each week of the month. Alternatively, an average can be taken of the trained staff count at the beginning and end of the month.

Using the data from the previous table, the calculation yields the following result:

$(20 \div 104) \times (12 \div 8) = 28.8\%$

Consequently, the call center has an annualized turnover rate of about 29 percent. While an overall annualized turnover rate is a useful number, it is of more value to further break down the number into internal/external, and voluntary/involuntary categories. Related term: Retention.

Two-Tier Architecture. A computing systems arrangement where functionality is split between two computing devices. At the client layer (usually a PC), presentation (GUI) and application level (business rules) reside. In the server, the application and data (database) reside. Application functionality can be split between the client and the server, or reside all in the client or all in the server. Compare with Three-Tier, N-Tier and Client/Server. (Vanguard)

Un-PBX. A term sometimes used for communications server. (Vanguard)

Unavailable Work State. An agent work state used to identify a mode not associated with handling telephone calls.

Unified Reporting. Data from different channels and systems are included on one reporting tool. This supports better analysis and decision-making in the organization.

Uniform Call Distributor (UCD). A simple system that distributes calls to a group of agents and provides some reports. A UCD is not as sophisticated as an ACD, and UCDs usually use simple hunt groups for call distribution. See Hunt Group.

Uniform Resource Locator (URL). The address for a Web page that is translated to an IP address.

Universal Agent. Also known as super agent. Refers to either: A) an agent who can handle all types of incoming calls, or B) an agent who can handle all channels of contact (e.g., inbound calls, outbound calls, email, text-chat, etc.).

Unix. A multiuser, multitasking operating system. Because it is written in the C language, UNIX is more portable (less machine-specific) than other operating systems.

Unstructured Interview. An interview that consists of random questions designed to gain insight into the candidate's suitability for the job. The questions are not documented in a standard interview guide. Instead, they are selected by the interviewer on the spot. See Structured Interview.

Upsell. A suggestive selling technique of offering more expensive products or services to current customers during the sales decision. The offer usually is based on relationships established between the customer's profile and the attributes of customers who have already purchased the products or services being upsold. Related terms: Customer Profiling, Customer Segmentation.

Upsell and Cross-Sell Ratios. This is the percentage of attempts to upsell or cross-sell that are successful. Upselling and cross-selling efforts should be more successful when they are part of a coherent customer relationship management strategy.

U

User-to-User Information (UUI). A method of passing information between communications systems via the D channel of an ISDN circuit. Information passed can be prompted digits, call identifiers, or custom application information. UUI is more widely used in multisite call center networking applications. (Vanguard)

Value Proposition. See Call Center's Value Proposition.

Variance Report. A report illustrating budget/cost objectives that look at the difference between projected and actual expenditures for various budget categories. Once a budget is created, controls need to be put in place. These controls provide information on the variance between actual results and the budget, and identify those areas where the variance exceeds expectations. Financial control reports provide call center managers with output results concerning expense performance. These outputs display results for the current month along with year-to-date summaries.

Besides an overall summary of department results, budget variance reports typically provide breakdowns on subcategories such as:

- Staff (agent) salary expenses
- Support staff expenses
- Telecom costs
- Technology charges (including maintenance)
- Rent and utilities
- Outside training charges
- Supplies and other office expenses

A typical budget variance report runs many pages, with the format broken down like this:

	Month				Year to Date			
	Budget	Actual	$ Variance	% Variance	Budget	Actual	$ Variance	% Variance
Salary								
Team 1	36,434	33,079	-3,355	-9.21%	101,497	94,331	-7,166	-7.06%
Team 2	39,502	41,441	1,939	4.91%	116,595	120,037	3,442	2.95%
Team 3	31,117	34,508	3,391	10.90%	95,021	102,595	7,574	7.97%
Team 4	34,049	35,089	1,040	3.05%	101,314	101,010	-304	-0.30%
Salary Subtotal	**141,102**	**144,117**	**3,015**	**2.14%**	**414,427**	**417,973**	**3,546**	**0.86%**
Building Expenses								
Rent	9,000	9,000	0	0.00%	27,000	27,000	0	0.00%
Utilities	3,988	4,161	173	4.34%	12,131	12,337	206	1.70%
Security	11,150	13,000	1,850	16.59%	33,450	37,150	3,700	11.06%
Building Subtotal	**24,138**	**26,161**	**2,023**	**8.38%**	**72,581**	**76,487**	**3,906**	**5.38%**
Total	**165,240**	**170,278**	**5,038**	**3.05%**	**487,008**	**494,460**	**7,452**	**1.53%**

These output reports are important in helping call center managers assess the financial performance of their organization. However, they do not typically provide any information concerning the reasons for the variance. An input report provides the manager with key information regarding the drivers of financial performance. An obvious input in a call center is contact workload. Minor fluctuations in projected workload vs. actual typically have little to no impact on staffing expenses. However, larger fluctuations can create a substantial gap between expectations and results. The following numbers are typical input drivers in a call center:

- Volume
- Average handle time
- Service level
- Average salary
- Adherence
- Turnover
- Support staff size
- Minutes of phone usage

Some of the above numbers have further subcategories that can form the basis for variance reports. One example is volume, which in many call centers is a function of the size of the customer base and the calling rate per customer. Average handling time (AHT) is another key example since volume and AHT forecast accuracy impact staffing levels about the same. Generating variance reports at this level provides further information on the cause of differences between actual and projected results.

An example of an operational input variance report for a few key indicators is as follows:

	Month				Year to Date			
	Budget	Actual	$ Variance	% Variance	Budget	Actual	$ Variance	% Variance
Call Volume	63,087	66,509	3,422	5.42%	194,507	208,429	13,922	7.16%
Membership	2,417,509	2,341,997	-75,512	-3.12%	2,357,914	2,302,816	-55,098	-2.34%
Calling Rate	2.61%	2.84%	0.23%	8.82%	8.25%	9.05%	0.80%	9.72%
AHT	326	337	11	3.37%	322	333	11	3.42%
Talk Time	287	292	5	1.74%	283	290	7	2.47%
After-Call Work	39	45	6	15.38%	39	43	4	10.26%
Average Salary								
CSR	12.48	12.63	0.15	1.20%	12.43	12.51	0.08	0.64%
Team Leader	14.27	14.42	0.15	1.05%	14.27	14.42	0.15	1.05%
Asst Sup	17.89	17.53	-0.36	-2.01%	17.61	17.48	-0.13	-0.74%
Supervisor	21.12	21.56	0.44	2.08%	20.97	21.11	0.14	0.67%
Staff Counts								
CSR	61	60	-1	-1.64%	62	61	-1	-1.61%
Team Leader	8	7	-1	-12.50%	8	8	0	0.00%
Asst Sup	4	4	0	0.00%	4	3	-1	-25.00%
Supervisor	4	4	0	0.00%	4	4	0	0.00%

Once the key input drivers are identified, reports should be created that provide information on driver results in comparison to expectations. Use these reports as the basis to create explanations of variances in financial results. They also provide the foundation for creating action plans to address performance problems. See Budget.

Video Display Terminal (VDT). Another term for computer monitor; a data terminal with a TV-like screen.

Vietnam Era Veterans Readjustment Act (U.S.). The Vietnam Era Veterans Readjustment Act of 1974 prohibits discrimination against Vietnam-era veterans by federal contractors.

Virtual Call Center. Also called distributed call center. Multiple networked call centers that operate as a single logical system even though they are physically separated and geographically dispersed. This permits economies of scale in call-handling, as well as supporting disaster recovery, call overflow and extended hours of coverage. Ability and degree of networking varies with system type, similarity of systems and approach to integration. It is enabled to varying degrees using network features, voice-switch features or CTI. (Vanguard)

Virtual Private Network (VPN). A method for using a public network (like the Internet) for a company's private business purposes. To address security, information is encrypted before being sent and then decrypted at the receiving site. (Vanguard)

Visible Queue. When callers know how long the queue that they just entered is, and how fast it is moving (e.g., they hear a system announcement that relays the expected wait time). Related terms: Invisible Queue, Queue.

Vision. Describes a future state of the organization in vivid, compelling terms. The organization's vision is a snapshot of the future. Vision is at the heart of great leadership because it allows leaders to communicate persuasively where the organization desires to go, and motivates everyone to work toward the same end. Core values, vision and mission are simply three interrelated components of defining and describing an organization's essence. Related terms: Core Values, Mission, Strategy.

Voice Authentication. See Speaker Verification.

Voice Extensible Markup Language (VXML). An emerging standard for developing voice-processing (IVR) applications with Internet and Web-based tools. The vision of VXML is that millions of Web developers will be able to develop IVR and speech recognition applications, based on a familiar programming format. (Vanguard)

Voice over Internet Protocol (VoIP). Transmitting voice conversations as packets of data from one communications device (voice switch, PC or IP phone) to another over a TCP/IP network. (Vanguard)

Voice Processing. An umbrella term that refers to any combination of voice technologies, including voicemail, automated attendant, audiotex, voice response unit and faxback. See Interactive Voice Response.

Voice Response Unit (VRU). See Interactive Voice Response.

Voice Switch. The PBX, ACD, Communications Server, Centrex, key system or other switching system for voice communications. (Vanguard)

Voicemail. Voicemail systems enable users to create, send, receive, listen to, edit and forward recorded voice messages.

VoiceXML (VXML). See Voice Extensible Markup Language.

Voluntary Turnover. See Turnover.

Wallboard. See Readerboard.

Wallet Share. Related to customer retention is wallet share, also called share of wallet. This refers to the amount of a customer's total spending that goes to your organization. Instead of focusing on capturing a percentage of the market, as in market share, the focus is on maximizing the amount of money spent by each customer. This is most often accomplished by diversifying the organization's products and services since, for most products and services, an individual customer will only need or want so much of the same thing.

Web Call. A voice call initiated by a customer from a company's Web site. Web calls can be accomplished in two ways: the caller can speak by VoIP over the Internet or be immediately called back over the PSTN. Regardless of calling method, the caller and agent speak while collaborating on a Web-based application. (Vanguard)

Web Call-Through. Using voice over Internet (VoIP) technology, the customer clicks on a button that establishes a voice line directly to the call center.

Web Callback. By clicking on a button, the customer lets the company know that he/she wants to be called back either immediately or at a designated time.

Web Collaboration. A broad term referring to the ability for an agent and customer to share content by pushing/pulling Web pages and/or whiteboarding and page markup.

Web Integration. Incorporating Web contact into the call center by providing access to an agent over the Internet when needed. Provides the customer with additional support, information and guidance during a self-service transaction. Can be enabled through text-chat or a Web call. Email is sometimes included offered as part of this integration. Often includes "co-browsing" or "pushing" Web pages to the customer. (Vanguard)

Web Self-Service Tools. Enable customers to receive information and answers to questions, place orders and view order status directly from the corporate Web site without contacting the call center for assistance. The key components of Web self-service include FAQs, interactive search engines, personal accounts, customized Web pages (that enable customers to update/change preferences), as well as "virtual assistants" (digital characters programmed with advanced artificial intelligence and that can interact in real-time with online customers via chat or voice). In addition to empowering customers to help themselves, Web self-service tools can capture a wealth of customer information that can be used to provide highly personalized support. See Self Service System.

Whisper Transfer. An IVR integration technique where the IVR temporarily connects to the agent and speaks the account number or other information before connecting the caller to the agent. Allows the agent to access information without the customer having to repeat information already entered into the IVR. Sometimes called "poor man's CTI." (Vanguard)

Wide Area Network (WAN). The connection of multiple geographically dispersed computers or LANs, normally using digital circuits. The device that connects A LAN to a WAN is usually a router. Related term: Local Area Network. (Vanguard)

Wide Area Telecommunications Service (WATS). WATS has become a generic term for discounted toll services provided by long-distance and local telephone companies.

Wireless Application Protocol (WAP). A carrier-independent protocol for wireless networks, designed to enable wireless users to access a new generation of multimedia and Web-based services. For updates on this specification, see www.wapforum.org.

Work Blending. The ability to dynamically and automatically allocate call center agents to any media, based on conditions in the call center and programmed parameters. Related terms: Blended Agent, Call Blending, Multimedia Routing and Queuing. (Vanguard)

Work State. An ACD-produced indicator of the status of a call center agent's activity or status. See Agent Status.

Workflow. A business application that enables work tasks to be executed consistently and thoroughly, driven by business rules. The movement of each task can be tracked throughout the duration of the process providing both current status and historical activity. Workflow management can be used to track contact-handling at specific stages or for the life of a contact. Workflow is an element of CRM solutions. (Vanguard)

Workforce Management System (WFMS). Software systems that, depending on available modules, forecast call load, calculate staff requirements, organize schedules and track real-time performance of individuals and groups. Workforce management can be performed for a single site or for networked sites. In a multisite environment, forecasting and scheduling may be performed at a central site or in a decentralized fashion at each site. Tracking and adherence monitoring is generally a local function.

At a basic level, workforce management systems provide automated support for four key processes in the call center – forecasting, staffing projections, scheduling and tracking:

- Forecasting is generally based on time series approaches that assess past patterns and trends and project them into the future. Generally, the user has a variety of options for overriding or changing projections and adding in judgmental criteria.

- The "engine" behind staffing projections is generally comprised of a set of Erlang calculations (including Erlang C and Erlang B) or modified Erlang calculations that compute staff and system capacity requirements. Some vendors also provide simulation capability for running complex scenarios.

- Scheduling is generally based on an iterative approach in the software that creates and organizes schedules based on user-defined parameters.

- Tracking and reporting provide the capability for users to compare actual results against projections in a real-time mode (tracking) and historically (reporting). Most WFMS not only track and report on volume activity, but also on handling time and adherence to schedule and absenteeism.

While a reduction in payroll expenses is typically the key benefit to a WFMS, most can also automate many other processes in a call center. Typical examples of additional functionality include the following:

- ACD integration
- Vacation approvals and administration
- Shift development
- Real-time adherence
- Meeting/break-time optimization
- Payroll system interfaces
- Networked site capabilities

These features either help to maximize the efficiency of the schedules developed (e.g., meeting/break-time optimization) or automate processes, such as vacation administration, which would otherwise be time-consuming. Some vendors have taken these concepts even further with functionality that includes skills-based scheduling, integrated forecasting and scheduling for multiple-access channels (email, text-chat, etc.), schedule viewing and shift changes/swapping via the Intranet. Related terms: Computer Simulation, Erlang B, Erlang C, Forecasting Methodologies, Queue Dynamics.

Workload. Often used interchangeably with call load. Workload can also refer to non-call activities. See Call Load.

World Wide Web (WWW). The capability that enables users to access information on the Internet in a graphical environment.

Wrap-Up. See After-Call Work.

Wrap-Up Codes. Codes that agents enter on their phones to identify the types of calls they are handling. The ACD can then generate reports on call types, by handling time, time of day, etc. Wrap-up codes are generally entered at the completion of each contact, although some systems enable agents to enter wrap-up codes while in talk time.

X-Axis. The horizontal axis on a graph or chart.

XML. See Extensible Markup Language.

Y-Axis. The vertical axis on a graph or chart.

Zip Tone. See Beep Tone.

The following sources were used in this project:

Incoming Calls Management Institute (ICMI)
410-267-0700
www.incoming.com
icmi@incoming.com

Most terms in the dictionary come from Incoming Calls Management Institute (ICMI), and ICMI research, seminars and publications. ICMI terms are unmarked. In addition to the original content produced for this publication, the following sources were used:

Advanced Workforce Management Web Seminar Series, presented by ICMI.

Call Center Coaching Web Seminar Series, presented by ICMI.

Call Center Forecasting and Scheduling: The Best of Call Center Management Review. Call Center Press (a division of ICMI, Inc.), 2000.

Call Center Monitoring Web Seminar Series, presented by ICMI.

Cleveland, Brad and Debbie Harne, Editors. *Call Center Customer Relationship Management Handbook and Study Guide.* Call Center Press (a division of ICMI, Inc.), 2003.

Cleveland, Brad and Debbie Harne, Editors. *Call Center Leadership and Business Management Handbook and Study Guide.* Call Center Press (a division of ICMI, Inc.), 2003.

Cleveland, Brad and Debbie Harne, Editors. *Call Center Operations Management Handbook and Study Guide.* Call Center Press (a division of ICMI, Inc.), 2003.

Cleveland, Brad and Debbie Harne, Editors. *Call Center People Management Handbook and Study Guide.* Call Center Press (a division of ICMI, Inc.), 2003.

Cleveland, Brad and Julia Mayben. *Call Center Management on Fast Forward: Succeeding in Today's Dynamic Inbound Environment.* Call Center Press, 9th printing, 2002.

Communicating the Value of the Call Center Across the Organization Web seminar, presented by ICMI.

Sources

Effective Leadership and Strategy for Senior Call Center Managers public seminar, presented by ICMI.

Effective Workforce Management, Step-by-Step Web Seminar Series, presented by ICMI.

Essential Skills and Knowledge for Effective Incoming Call Center Management public seminar, presented by ICMI.

Multichannel Call Center Study Final Report. Call Center Press (a division of ICMI, Inc.), 2001.

Results-Oriented Monitoring and Coaching for Improved Call Center Performance public seminar, presented by ICMI.

Workforce Management: The Basics and Beyond public seminar, presented by ICMI.

TARP
703 524 1456 (U.S. number)
www.tarp.com
info@tarp.com

TARP is a joint venture partner of ICMI, and provided terms related to customer loyalty and satisfaction. References appear as "(TARP)" at the end of applicable terms. Primary sources include:

Cleveland, Brad and Debbie Harne, Editors. *Call Center Customer Relationship Management Handbook and Study Guide.* Call Center Press (a division of ICMI, Inc.), 2003. Note: Some sections of this publication were produced in conjunction with TARP, and contain TARP material.

ICSA/TARP Benchmarking Study of Electronic Customer Service. TARP White Paper, www.tarp.com, March 2001.

Market Damage Model Overview. TARP White Paper, www.tarp.com, revised 2001.

Vanguard Communications Corp.
973-605-8000 (U.S. number)
www.vanguard.net
info@vanguard.net

Vanguard Communications Corp. is a joint venture partner of ICMI, and provided many of the terms related to technology. References appear as "(Vanguard)" at the end of applicable terms. Primary sources include:

Bocklund, Lori and Dave Bengtson. *Call Center Technology Demystified: The No-Nonsense Guide to Bridging Customer Contact Technology, Operations and Strategy.* Call Center Press, 2002.

Cleveland, Brad and Debbie Harne, Editors. *Call Center Operations Management Handbook and Study Guide.* Call Center Press (a division of ICMI, Inc.), 2003. Note: Some sections of this publication were produced in conjunction with Vanguard, and contain Vanguard material.

Understanding and Applying Today's Call Center Technologies, a public seminar developed and presented by Vanguard Communications Corporation and sponsored by ICMI.

Other Sources

The following additional sources were used, as noted in definitions related to specific terms:

DeNisi, Angelo, and Ricky Griffin. *Human Resource Management.* Houghton Mifflin Company, 2001.

Groppelli, A.A. and Ehsan Nikbakht. *Barron's Finance*, Fourth edition. Barron's Educational Series, 2000.

Kaplan, Robert S. and David P. Norton. *The Strategy Focused Organization.* Harvard Business School Press, 2000.

McCune, Jenny. "Thirst for Knowledge." *Management Review*, April 1999.

Read, Brendan. *Designing the Best Call Center for Your Business: A Complete Guide for Location, Services, Staffing, and Outsourcing.* CMP Books, 2000.

Reichheld, Frederick. *The Loyalty Effect: The Hidden Force Behind Growth, Profits, and Lasting Value.* Harvard Business School Press, 2001.

Solomon, Laurie. "What Every Trainer Needs to Know About How Agents Learn." *Call Center Management Review,* June 1999.

Sources

Treacy, Michael and Fred Wiersema. *The Discipline of Market Leaders.* Perseus Press, 1997.

Walton, John. *Strategic Human Resource Development.* Financial Times Management, 1999.

The International Customer Management Institute (ICMI) is one of the call center industry's most established and respected organizations. Founded in 1985, ICMI delivered the industry's first management-level conferences, educational programs and publications.

While ICMI's path-breaking work continues, the mission remains much the same: to provide resources and expertise that help individuals and organizations improve operational performance, attain superior business results and increase the strategic value of their customer contact services. Today's ICMI melds the traditional focus on consulting, training, and high-level engagement with UBM's strength in media and events to create a powerful one-stop-shop resource. Through the dedication and experience of its team, uncompromised objectivity and results-oriented vision, ICMI has earned a reputation as the industry's most trusted source for:

- Consulting
- Training
- Publications
- Events
- Professional Membership

Through constant innovation and research, ICMI's consulting and training services have become the industry's gold standard. ICMI publications, such as *Call Center Magazine* and *Call Center Management Review*, and events, including the Annual Call Center Exhibition (ACCE) and Call Center Demo and Exhibition conferences, continue to lead the industry. And ICMI's growing membership community now includes professionals representing organizations in over 50 countries.

How to Contact the Author

We would love to hear from you! How could this book be improved? Has it been helpful? No comments are off limits! You can reach us at:

Mailing Address:	ICMI Press
	102 South Tejon, Suite 1200
	Colorado Springs, CO 80903
Telephone:	719-268-0305, 800-672-6177
Fax:	719-268-0184
Email:	icmi@icmi.com
Web site:	www.icmi.com
Author email:	bradc@icmi.com

Order Form

QTY.	Item	Member Price	Price	Total
	Call Center Management On Fast Forward: Succeeding In Today's Dynamic Customer Contact Environment**	**$33.96**	$39.95	
	It's Better to be a Good Machine than a Bad Person: Speech Recognition and Other Exotic User Interfaces in the Twilight of the Jetsonian Age**	**$33.96**	$39.95	
	How to Build a Speech Recognition Application: A Style Guide for Telephony Dialogues	**$80.75**	$95.00	
	Customer Centricity through Workforce Optimization	**$29.71**	$34.95	
	Call Center Handbook Series A Career for the 21st Century** The Voice of Your Company: Conversational Skills for Customer Service Reps** Your Pivotal Role: Frontline Leadership in the Call Center**	**$11.01 ea.**	$12.95 ea.	
	Driving Peak Sales Performance in Call Centers**	**$33.96**	$39.95	
	Call Center Technology Demystified: The No-Nonsense Guide to Bridging Customer Contact Technology, Operations and Strategy**	**$33.96**	$39.95	
	ICMI's Call Center Management Dictionary: The Essential Reference for Contact Center, Help Desk and Customer Care Professionals**	**$21.21**	$24.95	
	ICMI's Pocket Guide to Call Center Management Terms**	**$5.12**	$5.95	
	ICMI Handbook and Study Guide Series Module 1: People Management** Module 2: Operations Management** Module 3: Customer Relationship Management** Module 4: Leadership and Business Management**	**$169.15 ea.**	$199.00 ea.	
	Topical Books: **The Best of *Call Center Management Review*** Call Center Recruiting and New Hire Training** Call Center Forecasting and Scheduling** Call Center Agent Motivation and Compensation** Call Center Agent Retention and Turnover**	**$14.41 ea.**	$16.95 ea.	
	Forms Books Call Center Sample Monitoring Forms** Call Center Sample Customer Satisfaction Forms Book**	**$42.46 ea.**	$49.95 ea.	
	Software QueueView: A Staffing Calculator CD ROM* Easy Start™ Call Center Scheduler Software CD-ROM*	**$41.65** **$254.15**	$49.95 $299.00	
	Call Center Humor: The Best of Greg Levin's "In Your Ear" Satire Columns, Volume 4**	**$8.45**	$9.95	
	The Call Centertainment Book**	**$7.61**	$8.95	
	Shipping & Handling @ $5.00 per US shipment, plus .50¢ per* item, $1.00 per** item and $2.00 per*** item. Additional charges apply to shipments outside the US.			
	Applicable State Sales Tax will be Applied			
	TOTAL (US dollars)			

Please contact us for quantity discounts. For more info on our products, please visit **www.icmi.com**